THE LONG WALK

Queenscliff to Adelaide

G.E. Morrison

ETT IMPRINT
Exile Bay

First published in Imprint Classics by ETT Imprint, Exile Bay 2025

Diary of a Tramp first published as by *The Leader* in 1880
The Traveller was first published by *The Leader* in May 1883

First electronic edition ETT Imprint 2025

Introduction © Alan Ventress 2025
This edition copyright © Tom Thompson 2025

Compiled by Tom Thompson

This book is copyright. A part from any fair dealing for the purposes of private study, research criticism or review, as permitted under the Copyright Act, no par may be reproduced by any process without written permission. Inquiries should be addressed to the publishers:
ETT IMPRINT
PO Box R1906
Royal Exchange NSW 1225
Australia

ISBN 978-1-923205-70-3 (paper)
ISBN 978-1-923205-71-0 (ebook)

Cover: G.E. Morrision, 18 years old, 1880

Cover design by Tom Thompson

The Long Walk

Introduction by Alan Ventress   5
The Long Walk   9
The Traveller:
Across the Australian Continent on Foot   63

George Ernest Morrison, aged 18, as photographed in 1880.

G. E. Morrison - A Very Long Walk

The early life of George Ernest Morrison has been overshadowed by his 20 years in China as a journalist for twenty years during a very volatile period in Chinese history. He arrived in what was then called Peking in 1897 and remained there for twenty years, earning the nickname Chinese Morrison.

Morrison was born near Geelong in 1862, so in 1879 he was a young man of 17 and approaching his 18th birthday in February 1880. He started what he called his Long Walk at the end of December 1879 and completed it in February 1880. His starting point was Queenscliff in Victoria and his destination was Adelaide, a distance of 752 miles or 1210 kilometres.

Morrison's diary of his walk gives us a candid look at the lives of the average Australians he met along the way and some of the adventures and difficulties he encountered. Morrison has a good eye for detail and lets the reader know exactly what he was carrying, what he was wearing and the food he consumed during his journey. It is a fact that is well known that places are remembered by what we ate and it was no different for Morrison in the late 1800s. It is hard to imagine that a current day hiker would consider such a journey with such a small amount of supplies and available cash which he calculates at 6 pounds 14 shillings and 6 pence. This amount could be calculated at around $1000 today. Nevertheless even at this level, S1000 for a two month hike of over 1000 kilometres is a significant achievement.

The roads, tracks and pathways Morrison traverses are generally in poor condition and there seems to be few signposts so he has to rely on the directions of locals to point him in the general direction of his destination. In addition some of the tracks are totally non-existent which involves what can only be described as bush bashing. The prospect of a journey today without a map or a handheld GPS would be unthinkable to most.

Morrison makes a point of noting the names of those he meets along the way, together with a brief overview of their lives and reasons for being where they are, giving us a brief window into lives which have long been forgotten. In many cases perhaps the only record of an individual's existence. The generosity of those he meets along the way is also always very apparent and Morrison is often given free accommodation and meals which invariably he graciously accepts. Though on one occasion he asks what the bill is, only to be told "What would he think of a man who had not seen anyone for six months if he charged for an overnight stay?"

Creeks, rivers and inlets do not appear to disturb Morrison's progress and he quickly either wades over them or commandeers a rowing boat to get over these obstacles with little concern on how the owner might feel when the boat is found to be missing and moored on the opposite bank of the river. It is apparent that Morrison is a fearless individual and possibly would not have been deterred, even by crocodiles if he were in tropical North Queensland instead of temperate Victoria and South Australia.

Some of the hotels where Morrison stayed were very poor and bordering on squalid, most notably The Lamb in Portland which was full of flies, which seems hardly surprising given the lack of cleaning in that establishment. The food he was offered left a lot to be desired too, cold fish, old bread and rancid butter, something only a young man with little choice on the road can accept. Some more modern country hotels are little better these days, a sign seen in Orbost recently, encouraging patrons to vomit into the cardboard boxes (provided) not into the hand basin.

One aspect of Morrison's long walk is naturally his constant need for water and the many times he must endure his walk without a drink or to take water from dubious sources, such as a swamp. He is also, on occasion, unable to help those he meets along the way who are craving a drink. Fortunately for him he does not succumb to the effects of poor quality water though he does appear to have a mild dose of food poisoning from a crayfish. A more severe case would have ended his walk.

The harshness of the environment he walks through coupled with the heat of the day, as he was walking in the hottest months of the year, makes Morrison's Long Walk especially noteworthy. He captures aspects of Australian life which on the surface appear to be quite different to life in Australia today, however fundamentally they are the same and very little has changed in the character of Australians since 1880 which I am sure Morrison would find gratifying.

Morrison's wanderlust returned and in December 1882 he set off on an exceptionally long walk, in essence following the route Burke and Wills had taken, but in reverse. His experiences were published in a short essay entitled **The Traveller: Across The Australian Continent on foot** which was published in *The Times* (Melbourne), a paper he subsequently worked for. The distances he travelled were extremely long and arduous, especially on foot and with the need to carry his own food and water through some of the harshest landscapes in Australia. Morrison once again proved his exceptional resilience, perseverance and strength of character by doing this journey. However, he was always modest about his achievements and never boasted about his remarkable walking ability. Morrison was also very flexible in his choice of work along the way and worked as a theatre entrepreneur, miner and draughtsman seizing every opportunity that presented itself. At this stage of his life he was in his early twenties and if he had done nothing more in his life it would have been regarded as a life well lived.

Alan Ventress

The Long Walk

Tuesday December 30, 1879

I left Queenscliff after an early lunch on Tuesday December 30th 1879 and it is my intention to endeavour to reach Bream Creek tonight, Swampy Creek tomorrow and then, by rising early and doing some hard walking, get into Lorne in time for my New Year's dinner.

My attire was the subject of flattery as regards its usefulness, laughter as regards its appearance. On my head I wore a peaked hat which is certainly more suited for cold weather, but as it is so made that at will I could cover all my face with it except my eyes. At Mama's request and sollicitation I got a sun shade which fits on to the cap and protects the back of the head. My clothing consisted of a thick armless woollen guernsey, my cricketing shirt and cricketing coat, serge trousers specially strengthened, comfortable socks and a light but strong pair of boots. As a protection against snakes I also wore leggings.

On my back I carried a famous knapsack of my own invention. It was made of strong canvas doubled next back, but of a single piece outside and it had a partition down it. It was kept on my back by straps passing round my shoulders and round my waist and on the outside of it there were two straps intended for carrying my coat if it should be too hot to wear it.

My knapsack contained the following articles: two loaves of bread, a well roasted boneless leg of mutton; half a pound of salt, $^{1/4}$ lb. pepper; 3 lemons. Two tooth brushes and a box of tooth powder, some rag, a towel, 5 pairs of socks, 2 cotton handkerchiefs, two silk do., some soap and oilsilk. Writing materials and a comb; a small quotation and a note book. In the strap going round my waist was stuck a tomahawk. The only thing I carried was a billy with another one fitting inside it and this contained four penny boxes of matches, a box of zinc ointment, some twine, lead pencils, some flannel bandage and some calico do. In one of my trouser pockets I carried a penknife, in the other my small chamois leather bag of money consisting of three one pound notes, two sovereigns, 10 half crowns, two shillings and 15 sixpences - altogether six pounds fourteen shillings and six pence.

I was accompanied to the Barwon Heads by Harry Adams who had kindly volunteered to see me off. My knapsack was very heavy and hurt my back dreadfully. A fisherman put me across the river and I landed at the Sheep Wash. I feel as I set off for Bream Creek what an arduous walk I have undertaken, but with God's help I hope to get there all right. I am directed to a high sand cliff in the distance which I am told overlooks Bream Creek. I get there, but find it doesn't; there is another about a mile further on, perhaps that is it; again I am wrong. Nothing daunted I make for a still more prominent hill, feeling sure that I must strike Bream Creek before I reach it, but alas disappointment again awaits me.

In despair I look around me. A road runs past a house in quite a different direction from where I am bound for, nevertheless I resolve to strike it. In doing so I have to cross a low marshy sort of plain covered with stunted bushes. I hear a rustling just beside me and a large snake doesn't glide quick enough away to prevent me having a good look - a shuddering look - at it.

I get a glass of water at the house and am told if I follow up the road I am now on and take the second turning to the left, it will take me to the mouth of Bream Creek. At the first turning I was done up. It was about 9 o'clock. With my knapsack for a pillow I lie down on the bare ground in the corner of a paddock, with a thorny hedge protecting me on two sides. The ground is prickly and cold. I try to go to sleep and commune with myself.

O Sleep, O gentle Sleep,
Nature's soft nurse, how have I frighted thee
That thou no more wilt weigh my eyelids down
And steep my senses in forgetfulness?

Just as I am getting unconscious I am aroused by a fearful din seemingly at my ears. It is a number of boys at a house near; one or two are singing the *Sweet Bye and Bye,* the rest keeping time with kerosene tins, boxes, sticks and cetera. In turn we hear the following tunes or mutilations (variations) thereof: *My Grandfather's Clock, Take it Bob, Hold the Fort, Bonnie Dundee, God Save the Queen* and others. At length I go off into a sort of dreamy unconsciousness and though I was very cold and uncomfortable all night, when I woke in the morning I felt refreshed.

I set off soon after daybreak for Bream Creek and walking there had a glorious view of the sun rising. I don't think I ever saw a more magnificent sunrise, though it betokened a warm day.

Following the directions received overnight I soon found myself at the mouth of Bream Creek. This creek was running out and as it was two foot deep I had to take off my boots and stockings. Fishing off the rocks were two lads. From them I learnt that the time was 7.30 and the tide was coming in.

A pleasant walk of four miies along the hard sand brought me to two deserted fishermens' huts. From a well near I got excellent water. By taking a line cross country I saved two miles in getting to Spring Creek. No less than six tents were pitched in a bend of the river. Spring Creek, though larger than Bream Creek, and just as salt, has its mouth always barred.

High tide prevented me walking round the beach to Swampy Creek so I had to take to the cliffs. After having something to eat an" boiling a billy of water I started. The cliffs here are magnificent. I have to walk along the edge and three hundred feet below me the sea curled round the rock and dashed against its feet.

Walking in such a way was very tiring and at the first opportunity --- at a gully or dry watercourse near a place called Benfeather's cottage a- bout three or four miles from Spring Creek - I went down on the beach and followed it for three or four miles till I came to a corner where I couldn't get round, so I had again to toil up the hills - this time a particularly steep one - and descend at the other side of the difficulty. I then kept the beach right to Swampy. I was much struck with the cliffs passed on route. Some would be rough and rugged, of a yellow colour, with no trees near them; others perfectly perpendicular with the lines of formation horizontal, perpendicular or vertical. In other places cliff would rise above cliff, bare before me, but wooded on their summit, till they seemed almost to reach the sky.

The prettiest sight however was where the cliff of immense height would be perpendicular and bare for one hundred feet or so and then would gradually shelve in a splendidly wooded incline down to the sea beach, or instead of shelving by gradual incline it would form a concave mass.

In many places the sea had hollowed out the cliffs at the base to a distance of several feet.

When boiling my billy at Swampy Creek two young residents in a house near came down to see me and their interest evinced itself more practically in the shape of a lent blanket, overcoat and pillow. My bed was in a clump of trees on the river's bank and lying awake with strange noises going on all around me I see the Old Year 1879 out and the New Year 1880 in.

In the morning when I get up half an hour before sunrise, I find I am wet through; my boots and leggings especially are soaking. My feet also are raw and in no fit state do I feel for a long walk. From the top of the hill overlooking Swampy Creek I get a most glorious view. Away to the left stretched ranges of beautiful wooded hills and as the mist still hung over the valleys it looked as if a snowy lake nestled in snug places among the hills.

At the foot of the hill I am on, lies Swampy Creek placid in its smoothness and away beyond it I see the coast and cliffs extending miles upon miles. To my right lies the sea bank. Behind me tower still higher hills. I resolved instead of taking the ordinary road to Ayrey's Inlet through the ranges to try the old track which keeps near the coast.

I start and am led by the road a most delightful walk. The sea is in sight all the time and as the coast bends round a great deal I am enabled to distinguish Eaglehawk Peak and Loutit Bay. The latter place gets more and more distinct till I can see the houses and fancy I distinguish the new hotel at the Point.

The road I have taken is longer and more tedious than the one I went by last time. By cutting away at right angles I come out into the open on the bare hill opposite Berthon's house. Airey's Inlet is not a bay formed by the sea, though it may have been once. The inlet is a plain of low lying country covered with dead timber on one half, but cultivated in the half next the sea coast. Serpentining through it in a most extra- ordinary manner is Airey's Inlet Creek. A large gap in the hills has been made by nature to enable the river to enter the sea, but for reasons best kn9wn to itself it has failed to take advantage of this. On one of the gray hills overlooking the plain and fronting the sea is seen a square house made of white stone. This is Mr. I.R. Hopkins holiday residence. I am very thirsty. It is now 8 a.m. There is a creek five miles round the beach. I hurry there, have a billy of tea, then going round a little further I take to the hills and follow the telegraph line over the tops of the hills. I again descend. A wash in the Reedy Creek and I start for Lorne which I reach by 3.30. Mount Joy's is very full. In the evening I go up to the Pacific Hotel to see Ted Nicholls. He shows me over it. It is magnificently furnished, equal to anything I have ever seen.

After New Year's dinner I resolved to sleep out. Mrs. Mountjoy lent me blanket, mattress and pillow, Mr. Gerrard a waterproof. I spend an enjoyable night in the bathing house. Next morning after breakfast I start for Apollo Bay.

I had ordered a roast leg of mutton weighing 4 lbs. Judge of my disgust when a boiled leg, weighing nine pounds made its appearance. On my refusing it, Mountjoy said there was only occasion to take enough for two meals as I could easily get to Apollo Bay that night. Accordingly I only took a couple of packets of sandwiches.

After tiresome jumping over rocks arrive at the Cumberland, having passed the St George and Sheoak. Arduous climbing for four miles took me to Jamieson's River - a creek very similar to the Cumberland and in a most picturesque situation. The whole of this stage was round the base of huge Mt. Defiance and I thought what a happy name it had. Another rest at the Jamieson and then a quick walk - though hard on my sore feet - brought me to the Wye. This is a remarkably picturesque river, having towering and splendidly wooded hills rising from its banks.

Saturday Jan. 3rd.

Here I found camped two men, Philip Henderson and Bob Straw, who had started from Lorne three hours before me. As it was very late in the day and I was very leg-weary I resolved to camp and go to Apollo Bay tomorrow with them. We fitted up a mia-mia, lit a glorious fire and I slept like a top; the others found it too cold. During the night we heard the lowing of wild bulls, the howling of wild dogs and the braying of native bears. We lit a glorious fire in front of our sleeping place and at 1.45 we got up, got warm and got back to bed again.

We started for Apollo Bay about half past seven. Four miles uninteresting walking over the hard but smooth rocks brought us to the Kennet, a fine large creek, but unfortunately salt and full of kelp. Henderson tried his hand at fishing, but unsuccessfully.

We still kept along the beach till we came to another creek about two miles on. We had been told to leave the coast when we came to a creek about two miles from the Kennet and if we saw a track up the hill to follow it and it would take us over the top of the Paton round Cape Paton. Well, here was the creek two miles from the Kennet and in front of us rose a clearly defined track up the hill. Without the slightest hesitation we went up it and in five minutes we were brought up at another creek. Here I found a flask of brandy. We now knew without a doubt that we had come to the Paton, so before starting we took a good rest.

After one continuous climb for an hour one of my companions thought that we had come to a track which we should take to the left. Accordingly we left the telegraph line and worked our way through thick scrub to the sea cliffs and we forced our way round these hills till we came onto the proper track, which we ought to have taken. The narrow path took us down and up delightful hills and across beautiful little fern tree gullies. Eventually we emerged into the open, having gradually descended down the narrow hills at the mouth of a creek.

Here we camped for dinner. We now knew that we were on'y ten miles from Apollo Bay, so started off joyfully to walk it. It was certainly the longest ten miles I ever walked in my life and took us five hours exclusive of stoppages. We walked today twenty-three miles. We passed thirteen creeks of fresh water and at each creek the scenery was more beautiful than at the others. The hills, though always very similar in their appearance never tire the eye nor become monotonous. As we are walking along tired and noiselessly Henderson jumps back excitedly, calling 'A snake, there's a snake, I see a snake'. Mr. Straw did perhaps the fastest retrograde twenty five yards ever seen, but he wasn't frightened, only alarmed. After a desperate and dangerous fight of half an hour with the snake we succeed in killing it. Its colour was something similar to the beach and I question if it wasn't harmless.

The name Apollo, though properly applied to the bay, has been transferred to the township. Consisting of one house and a pigswe, it is situated on a grassy flat fronting the sea and protected by hills. Close beside the house runs the river Barrum. The owner of the house, Cowood is line repairer from here to Lorne and is also operator at the telegraph station.

He had a telegraph for me from Stewart McArthur from Camperdown to the following effect: "Cannot keep cliffs from Otway to Gibsons. Track through bush. Do not attempt without guide or direction". I cannot understand what is meant. I am not due at Gibson's till the 8th, but at my present rate of travelling I shall get there on the 6th and if I lose myself nobody can be anxious for a day or two.

Stopping at Cowood's are two gentlemen who are on an excursion something like mine, only a pleasure one. They are Kermot and Gregory, two celebrated men; the former a lecturer on Civil Engineering at the Melbourne University, the latter on Common Law.

I had a glorious tea. My companions are going to stop here and tomorrow I shall go on with them as far as the Parker at least.

After many delays in saddling the pack horse etc., we set off. See us on the road: Mr. Gregory, a short broad-shouldered man with a long beard, slight stoop and handsome face, wearing a helmet hat; the very type of an explorer, leading. Myself in full war paint with bare arms next and Mr. Kernot, fairly tall, with a very round back, concave breast, narrow shoulders, knock knees, red nose and spectacles leading a packhorse. This horse is a perfect wonder of a traveller. He has climbed hills whereon the foot of horse has never before alighted, he has jumped over rocks never before seen by horse's eyes and what is more wonderful has turned somersaults down hill without hurting either himself or pack.

These two travellers do not much believe in roughing it. In the pack which consists of four large bags of canvas they carry every luxury from a tent to lime juice, sweet biscuits and figs.

Our route took an upward turn for miles and miles and following along we came into sight of the sea at Blanket Bay. Previous to this on the top of a high hill I spied a snake. In deliberating how we were to kill it it slipped into a log and we were delayed half an hour getting it, much to Mr. Kernott's disgust. It was only by luck we did dislodge it after all. I could clearly see disappointment in the physiognomy of its countenance as it spat, jumped and got killed at the same moment. Imagine the poor thing's feelings, whilst laughing in its sleeve at our hacks at the wrong limb, on being suddenly disturbed by a pointed stick. If it had kept quiet it would. even then have been safe, but it so boiled over with indignation that it couldn't hold itself and came out. A whack with a stick ended the fun.

From Blanket Bay we kept a well beaten dray path to the Parker, a beautiful river with a rustic bridge. Here I left my companions and went on alone. On rounding a hill I saw what looked like a church on the top of a hill. I made my way to this and was welcomed in most hospitably by Kelsall, the telegraph operator. He was most cordial, gave me a good tea and a shakedown on the sofa.

Next day, Monday, in the morning I was shown round. Visited the caves and limestone grottoes and went up the lighthouse. The man in charge showed us the revolving apparatus. The light is called a revolving light of the first order, transmitting a flash once every minute. There are twenty-one lamps and it takes seven lamps to make a flash, so it will be perceived that the whole affair turns round in three minutes. The lighthouse is very short and stumpy-looking, but this gives additional strength. The walls are five feet thick and the tower is round.

The only residents on the Cape which is the southernmost part of Australia are those who have to be there in an official capacity, such as the telegraph operator, the man in charge of the lighthouse and his assistants.

On taking leave of Kelsall I, of course, asked him what the bill was. He seemed quite annoyed at my doing so and asked me what I should think of a man who expected to be paid for a night's board and lodging by the only stranger he had seen for six months. His last few words raised my respect for him.

Monday 5th January

At three in the afternoon I left Cape Otway for Glenample, distant forty miles. I had appointed to sleep that night at a hut about eight miles from Cape Otway with a man who could tell me the track to Glenample. Accordingly I made for this hut. Having followed the coast line for three or four miles over the hills, I came to the river Aire. From where I stood on the top of the high sea bank I had a fine view of the river. At first sight it looked like an immense bay of bright sand with a silvery thread of water glistening under the lofty bank at the other side of the sand bay. The water was only two or three feet deep so I had no difficulty in getting across. My directions were to keep to a fence running parallel to the coast and to follow it until the hut stood before me. I followed it and shortly it turned away at right angles, yet still I kept on till I was abruptly brought up by the valley of the Ford, a stream tributary to the Aire. By keeping along the edge of this valley I came within sight of the hut, but on going up to it nobody was in.

As there was an hour or two of daylight, I, to pass away the time, walked up to the sea cliffs and followed them back again to the fence. The next time I got to the hut the man was there whom I expected.

Tuesday Jan. 6th.

That night I slept like a top. The next morning at 7.30 I started. The man, Jim Anderson, said I would see a track going up a hill and I was to follow that to Princetown. Over the hills to the river Johanna, previous to which I had crossed a small creek, and once beyond the Johanna and up a sand hill or two I got on to the track. It was just a narrow footpath eighteen inches wide and I couldn't expect it to be very clearly defined, as it had only once been crossed within the preceding twelve months. It first kept along the edge of the cliffs, but gradually edging off to my astonishment, it struck clean away into the forest, apparently on the top of a dividing range. After walking twelve miles or so in this direction without hardly seeing the sun, the foliage being so dense as to completely cover the path, all of a sudden, as it seemed to me, it turned gradually round and made for the coast through forest characterised by larger trees, but not such a dense undergrowth. This made the track harder to distinguish than before and often when it branched into two or three narrow paths I was in dread lest I should take a wrong turning and get off the proper road. I never once hesitated, but always went straight ahead and to this fact I owe my getting to the Gellibrand that night.

  I feel now what a dangerous walk it was; in fact it almost makes me shudder to think how easily I could have left the path for may be death. I calculated that I had walked about twelve miles in this other direction and I was beginning to get anxious lest I had been misinformed as to the distance. I was also very thirsty as I had not seen a drop of water since leaving the Johanna and being thirsty of course I couldn't eat arid consequently was weak. At length I fancied somehow or other instinctively that I was not very far from the sea. Seeing some green shrubs like hops which I have never seen except near the sea raised my drooping hopes and after keeping an imaginary track for a short time longer (I had completely lost the bush track) came out on the summit of a hill from which I could see the sea. Tracks - cattle - ran about in every direction. I took one which seemed to lead in the direction I wanted to go. This I followed without stopping for rest (I was so thirsty) for a distance of five or six miles - killing a snake basking in the track - till it took me out fair on to a bald hill close to the sea from which I could see the coast for miles along. It was very hot so, I lay down for a bit in the sun. Getting up I saw in the distance a sort of hill such as are usually at the mouth of rivers and resolved to make for this feeling confident the Gellibrand must be near it. The cattle track still led me and it gradually became more well beaten, till I saw a cleared place to which it was going (They were on different hills separated by a deep ravine) to my great joy I discovered a nice cottage, empty; and from an old barrel half full with rusty water I had a glorious drink. This was about half past five p.m. Ten hours is a long time to go without water, walking all the time and I suffered greatly.

  Set up now I went on my way. At another hut I met a young fellow and from him I learnt that the river which I now saw was the Gellibrand and that if I couldn't see anybody who would take me over in a boat he would be going across on horseback in an hour and then I could navigate it on his horse.

As I expected, nobody was about, so I waited for this verdant youth and in a couple of hours or so, about 8 o'clock, he turned up. The river was still too deep, so another long delay ensued. In about half an hour I grew impatient and the river having gone down about two inches we resolved to try it. Accordingly I mounted up behind. The horse was got under way and apparently made up its mind to take a header. The owner encouraged his vehicle to further efforts, 'Gee Woa, Get along with you, you fool. Won't I give it you when I get you on dry land etc. The horse refused to go a step further and stood there with its forelegs and chest in the water and its hind legs on dry land. I swore that if anybody got ducked it would be the driver and whilst urging him to propel his steed, the latter turned sharp round and came out on to dry land.

It was now quite dark and it was necessary to hurry if I wanted to get in to Mrs. Gibson's before they had shut up. I told the grinning idiot to cross when he could and I would go for a boat hunt. I followed the bank of the river up a good distance and fortunately came across a boat with two oars in it. I put myself across the river and then rode behind the chap on horseback up to Mrs. Gibson's. I was dead beat and nearly killed with jolting. Only one light was visible. I gave a timid knock at the door. A lady's voice replied 'Who's there?' My nervous response gained me admittance and after a most hospitable reception, and a good tea went to a warm bed. The total distance I had walked today was thirty-five miles.

Next morning, Wednesday, I didn't get up till late, I was so tired, and after breakfast talked with a young lady, a Miss Jessie Curdie, second daughter of Dr. Curdie of Tandarook, till dinner. She is five feet four inches, eight stone six pounds, with a good figure, pleasing face, nice voice and most fascinating manners.

Mrs. Gibson is very kind. The house is a stone one and is situated on the sea side of a hill sloping upwards to the sea bank. The front view takes in the country as far as the eye can reach towards Camperdown etc.

In the afternoon went down on the beach with Miss Curdie. Mr. Gibson has had cut in the perpendicular face of the cliff stone steps leading down to the beach and also has had excavated a famous tunnel

Cape Otway (above) and Blanket Bay (top) as Morrison would have seen it.

cut through the solid rock of a headland to make accessible another stretch of beach beyond. The cliffs all about here and for miles round are perfectly perpendicular, at places having immense gorges, also with perpendicular sides, running into the land and nearly always washed by the sea waves.

The most peculiar characteristic, however, is the number of immense rocks, or rather detached cliffs, standing right away from the land and surrounded with reefs, all about the coast. Many of these must be the size of a large church and of course have never been climbed.

Thursday, Friday, Saturday, Jan. 8-10th.

Thursday was a rainy day. About 3.30 in the afternoon I saw two horsemen coming from the direction of Camperdown. Shortly we made out these to be Stewart McArthur, and Bill Scott. The former was much surprised to see me. He didn't expect me till Friday.

Friday. Stewart went with Mr. Gibson to muster cattle and in the afternoon we went for a drive, S., Miss C. and I and Mr. S. riding round the coast and up to the Sherbroke. S. drove two ponies and they went fine.

Saturday. S. again mustering. Bill and I walked across to the sea, him carrying a gun with us. We saw a swan on the river. I sculled Bill up across, landed him. He stalked the swan, fired. Swan lay down. Bill congratulating, lights his pipe. Swan winks and flies off.

In afternoon Miss C. and S. drive, B. and I rode to Gellibrand. In evening wrote to Norman and Ted Nicholls.

Sunday. Again up late. Loafed in morning. Out on ponies in afternoon. One resolutely refused to go. In evening had a goat hunt. Stewart captured a little black one, but we had to let it go.

Monday. Beautifully hot. All up early. Stewart again at ponies - no good. In morning all rode over to the wreck. A delightful bathe in the Sherbroke: Saw lots of ducks.

Tuesday. Warm, windy and cold. Stewart and Bill Scott went away, taking with them the two ponies which S. is going to break in at home. About dinner time Mr. and Mrs. Begg of Ham. Acad. and G. Tait turned up. In afternoon went across to Gellibrand, a very pretty river. The view, with the river lying placid before me the low sea bank on the one side and huge Point Ronald opposite casting a shadow on the water with the sun just sinking behind it, was delightful. Had a row, very windy. In the evening service in the dining room. This morning Mr. Tait and all went again to the beach and they all went away about dinner time. Walked across to the wreck and took stock.

WRITTEN AT THE BACK OF THE DIARY NOTEBOOK

The gorge into which Tom Pearce and Miss Carmichael were washed is about one hundred and fifty yards to the right, that is the W. of where the *Loch Ard* struck. The Gorge running in first has a narrow opening which gradually widens till it is met by a headland running out from the land which divides it into two other gorges, the W. one being ever so much longer and deeper than the eastern one. At the furthest end of both these gorges there is a cave in which can be found fresh water.

The celebrated cave, however, is just round the first corner to the W. arriving in from the sea. It runs straight out in the direction of the sea for a distance of seventy-five yards. The whole of the gorge is apparently very shallow and there is a fine broad beach. Each of the sub-gorges is covered with shrubs and stunted bushes that have taken root in the sand.

The beach is accessible only by means of steps cut down the headland into the W. gorge and it was at the extremity of the headland, also on the W. that Tom Pearce scaled. The tree that Miss Carmichael hid herself under is now a single stem of a beech tree and is at the foot of the steps. The caves are very pretty, of lime formation, water dripping through the ceiling having formed pretty little stalactities. They are very cold and are said to be the home of bats. The smaller gorges are covered with wreckage and a fine spar was on the beach. Strange to say, this was the only gorge for miles where a human being could be washed up in safety.

The graveyard containing three tombstones is on the face of the hill overlooking the gorge. The greatest width is about fifty yards.

Arthur George Townshend Mitchell June 1st 1878, aged 26.

In Memoriam of Reginald Jones, youngest son of Francis and Clara Jones, Blackheath, Kent. Drowned in the *Loch Ard* June 1st 1878, aged 26 years

"Shall not the Judge of all the earth do right"

Sacred to the memory of Mrs. Eva Carmichael and Miss Raby Carmichael, whose bodies lie beneath. Also in remembrance of Dr. Evory Carmichael, Misses Margaret and Annie Carmichael; Masters Evory and Thomas Carmichael.

All of whom were lost in the calamitous wreck of the *Loch Ard* Saturday June 1st, 1878.

This stone is erected by Eva and William Carmichael, the former of whom was most miraculously preserved.

In affectionate remembrance of their deceased parents, brothers and sisters.

About a quarter of a mile to the W. of the Loch Ard Gorge is the famous blowhole. This is an immense pit in the ground, sixty yards long ten-thirty broad and c. fifty feet deep;, in shape similar to the gorges on the sea coast, except that it communicates with the sea by a huge subterranean tunnel over one hundred yards long. It seems to run still further inland underground, but it cannot be known with certainty; the waves dash into this blowhole and go roaming on into the other tunnel with a surging roar and splashing round that can be heard some way off. To fall in would be certain death.

About a hundred yards to the left is the gorge, a very broad and shallow one, near which the *Loch Ard* struck. In the entrance to this gorge, with part in the gorge, but the greater portion outside, runs a long narrow very lofty detached cliff. On a part of this in the gorge, on a level piece of rock just covered with water and which seems to form part of the pedestal of the cliff itself, the *Loch Ard* struck. In low water there is a beach in the gorge, but in rough weather the sea licks the rock to the height of seven or eight feet. The cliff or rock has an immense tunnel in it, almost detaching one end running parallel to the shore. At the mouth of this the *Loch Ard* struck.

Thursday Jan 15th

A lovely day. I say goodbye to Mrs Gibson with many thanks for the great hospitality she has shown me. I start away about 11 a.m. My road of course, as far as the Sherbroke is over the bald hills by the track which I have crossed often lately.

The Sherbroke is about four miles from Glenample and though a rather large river, is very uninteresting Having crossed at the bar I had to climb the usual high loose sand hill which marks the mouth of the river. This one though was exceptionally high.

At the top of the hill I again got on the road and followed it for four miles, always being near the sea. The coast, it seems, never varied. There were the same high sandstone cliffs, the same detached rocks and the same uninteresting bald hill slopes.

Port Campbell I came upon quite unexpectedly. I could see before ascended the final hill, houses away up a river, but I didn't know till coming down the hill I came upon a large house, evidently a store, that the bay I saw was Port Campbell and the creek was Campbell's Creek.

The scenery about was a great change from the everlasting bald prospect. The bay is broad and deep and runs in a good distance. The water in it is very deep and there is excellent anchorage. It is not, however, a safe port, being too much exposed to the south and S.W. winds and there is also some difficulty in getting into it, owing to a reef of rocks which runs out from the east extremity to a distance of a mile.

The bay is brought to a standstill by a low sand hill, though the valley of the creek, a valley about as broad as the port, itself, runs away between high hills as far as you can see.

On the W. shore is the wreck of the *Napier* and one of its boats is lying on the beach. A man intends to navigate this boat round to Geelong.

Besides the unfinished store above mentioned, there are two houses on the face of the hill overlooking the point on the E.

Between the Sherbroke and Port Campbell are two little creeks from which you can get drinkable water.

On leaving the Port I kept along the edge of the cliffs for some time, till the walk became so laborious that I cut away to the N.W. and fell in with the road again. The scene never varied. Away to my right were scattered clumps of trees usually near springs; to my left were bald hills covered with stunted bushes. This was for five miles. Then the country became more thickly timbered with wretched wattles, and the she-oak made its appearance. A gorge here, near a fence, was one of the finest I have ever seen. In shape it was a Port Campbell, in appearance it was like where the *Loch Ard* was wrecked.

From the appearance of the coast I inferred I was getting near some large river, sandy hills having taken the place of the previous bald ones. I did not, however, expect to come upon such a large lake as I did. It stretched away out of sight up to my right and from where I stood it seemed to be about a mile across.

From a house near, I was supplied with tea and then made my way along the shore to the mouth. This, never very broad, was at present bar· red by a ridge of sand, which appears to be the dividing ridge, having on the one side the lake and on the other the bay-shaped arm of the sea. The latter is very shallow, abounds with rocks and is utterly unnavigable. On the eastern shore lies the wreck of the *Young Australia* (below, 1872), once notorious, when it had the name of *The Carl* for the kidnapping adventures of Dr. Murray.

Running out from this shore into the sea is a low sandy spit, and at the furthest extremity of this is a rock named the Schomberg (sic) rock which marks the spot where a vessel of the name of Schomberg was wrecked.

On the lake or inlet were an immense number of swans. In one mob quite close I counted 157. The W. side of the bay that forms an entrance into the Curdie's inlet is remarkably rocky and studded with reefs.

The two houses at the point belong the one to Mrs. Hamilton, the other to Mrs. Robertson. I slept at the latter and had breakfast at the former. The distance from Mrs. Gibson's to Port Campbell is eight miles and from Port Campbell to Curdie's Inlet seven miles.

Leaving about 10 I still kept on the road and my attention was first drawn to a deep bay with little gorges running out from it into the land all round, like pendants from a necklace. The cliffs are low, round at the summit, of sandstone formation, jagged front and the majority are undermined. The country is barren and undulating. Every here and there water has collected in a hollow of the ground and then become overgrown with weeds. I must have passed fifty or sixty of them. Stretching away to my right the country seemed to keep the same height and was covered with forests of young timber. To my left the hills were quite bare.

Walking along every now and then you catch a glimpse of the inhospitable coast. Always the water-washed cliffs, with the huge detached rocks and sea dashing round them. I pass by the first house I come to and keep on over a sandy road till I come to a large house standing among a lot of ferns. I feel sure this is Irvine's and go across to see. On my telling my name he asked me in to dinner. Before doing so he took me across to show me the bay of islands. There is nothing very remarkable in this. Just an inlet divided with lofty detached cliffs. The centre one of all is called Lot's Wife. On the face of the rocks which we go down onto the beach, were cut the names of a number of fellows I know: I.I.A., N.H.R., W A.T., W.S.

Mr. Irvine says I am uneducated because I do not go in for Poetry, Sketching and Phrenology. He shows me original specimens of the two former and they excite my admiration. He tells me he looks at everything in the humorous light and versifies after the same style as Mark

Twain in *The Innocents Abroad*. My head is examined. I have strong moral character, never swear, tee-totaller, and keen sense of the ridiculous. Have no amativeness, combativeness, but strong religious feelings (This bump is at the side of my head and has been there ever since Toppy Longden's nose was broken). I would make a good parson or a merchant as I have a good business head, am steady and of sedentary inclinations. There is no use my trying to be a doctor as I have neither courage, energy, endurance, determination or self esteem. Have great affection for animals no destructiveness, am remarkably good-tempered and never subject to obstinacy.

The road still was through the same monotonous country, flat and bare. On coming to a place called Dancey's section, the road suddenly turns to the right to save some heavy sand and too close proximity to the cliffs. I kept the old track which is much the shorter and which took me past a number of cultivated paddocks till I got into the road again. A mile or two further on I came to a sly grog shanty, where I got a bottle of poisonous beer. Taking the second turning to the left I came to a house from which I was directed to Mr. Wilson's where I intended to stay the night. The rabbits were running about in swarms. On presenting my letter of introduction from Irvine I was most hospitably invited in and spent a very enjoyable evening. There are three brothers and a sister and they are well-to-do people.

Saturday January 17th.

Reaping was just going on. I had walked today about eighteen miles, six miles to Irvine's, ten to Mrs Palmer's and two to Wilson's. Saturday had a slight tendency to be wet and I had my misgivings when I started to walk the twelve miles to Warrnambool.

Mr. Wilson's house is some distance from the sea coast, though pretty near the main road to Warrnambool. I learn it is shorter to keep to the coast, so gradually edge across, jumping any amount of fences and crossing fields of stubble. At the foot of the Wilson's is a large swampy tract of ground which gradually merges into a large lake called Lake Bolan and at the furthest end of this is a fellmongery. I got onto the line of hills between this lake and the coast and kept it without deviation for eight or nine miles. The west hills gradually become lower till they seem to run down into the sea. Quite close to me is Warrnambool on this sandy sort of ledge.

I now turn down to my right and strike the main road. From here the road is very pretty with the Hopkins in the foreground and the tree-surrounded houses on its banks. The road takes me to the Hopkins Bridge where I have dinner and which is one hundred and eighty yards long. In an hour after I walk into Warrnambool, My unusual garb excites astonishment in the minds of the people and a feeling that I am ridiculous in myself, so that I lose no time in allaying both.

I try to get a map; cannot. Also find there are no letters. Warrnambool is a very lively looking place with cabs and exceptionally fine hotels.

I am again on the main road, this time bound for a Mr. McLaws to an adopted daughter of whom I have a letter of introduction. Walking on a hard metal road is very tiring, uninteresting and irritating. Mr. Rutledge's station is on both sides of me, splendidly grassed and watered by water pumped from some underground reservoir. About seven miles from Warrnambool, from an innkeeper named Johnstone, I am directed to Mr. McLaw's. Leaving the metal path, I cut across fields to a lofty hill with a telegraph line on the top. From the top of this a curious view met my eyes. Below me was a lake about six miles round and almost circular, with a lofty range of hills sloping gradually down to the banks all round, except in one part where the banks were low. In the middle of this lake, in fact taking up almost all but a narrow strip round, was a curious conglomeration of mountains forming an island. This mountain In is called the Tower Hill Mount and the lake is the Tower Hill Lake. The water is covered with weeds, there being only one bare patch opposite the low bank. About a mile round on the edge of the lake, that on the top of the lofty bank, I see a large stone house. I go up to it. A dry-looking girl comes to the door and I present my letter to Miss Love. She says in reply 'What's this about?' 'Read it and see', was the answer. She did so, then went inside and had a consultation and I am invited in.

Living here and owning the place is a kind old man, a retired public- an, Mr. David McLaws. Having no children of his own and his wife being dead, he has adopted three sisters and one brother called Love. I was told by Mr. Begg (who gave me the letter of Introduction) that the girls were rather colonial, so I did not expect much. They were the most ridiculously loud gawks I ever met. The quantity of 'H's dropped by the two younger was amply compensated for by the extraordinary rapidity of manufacture of them by the eldest sister. Their names were Lizzie, Maggie and Teeny, short for Christina. The second one is engaged to a draper's assistant. In return for Mr. McLaws keeping them, they are his servants, do the washing, cooking etc.

Twenty acres of potatoes and wheat. Behind it is the village of Koroit and the background is the forest. The land is very valuable, fifty pounds or sixty pounds an acre. Mc Law is benevolence itself. He came to the colony in 1841, is a carpenter by trade and was for years an hotel keeper in Belfast. He bought his present farm in 1852 and is now a wealthy man. His house is very well furnished. His right leg was broken thirty years ago and then wrongly set. It is now most painful to look at and the owner is lame.

I left well after dinner and walked round the lake until I got into a road which took me on and on till I eventually got out on to the low sandy coast hills. I then went on to the beach and walked barefoot as far as Belfast. The sea was out and the beach fine and hard. The rocks are large black boulders and the scenery similar to going to the Barwon Heads. When near a land mark I came over the ridge and walked along the road to Belfast, crossing by a bridge the river Moyne. I saw two men and a goose and am stopping at the Caledonian Inn, a second rate affair. Between Warrnambool and Belfast the bay is called Port Fairy.

The river Moyne before entering the sea forms into two branches enclosing an island. The eastern branch is navigable for small lighthouse. Belfast is very dull. I saw the Bank of Australasia, a fine two-storied bluestone building covered with ivy, at the corner of two streets, opposite the Stag Hotel.

I had a yarn to Deane, a police constable who was concerned with the Loch Ard. The best hotel is the Star of the West and the one I am stopping at is about the worst.

I had breakfast at 6.30 and started away about 7.00. My bill is four shillings. From Belfast to Portland is forty-three miles. I follow the main road and telegraph poles for twelve miles till I get to Yambuk and was within a mile or two of the coast all the time. The line of hills on my left was sparsely wooded. Lying dead in the middle of the road

I passed a snake. I suspect it was a tiger snake.

Yambuk is a small straggling bush township with a hotel or two, a couple of stores, a church, schoolhouse and post office. I buy some dinner. I do not leave the main road for two and a half miles when I turn left to get on a track running near the coast. *En route* I cross the Eumerella on a wooden bridge with stone entrances. This river is hardly distinguishable being thickly overgrown with rushes. The only clear patch to be Seen was under the bridge. The water is drinkable. The river drains a sort of extensive marsh covered with coarse grass and thistles and there are a many houses about. I had been for some time steadily making my way towards the coast and when I got onto a high ridge I came in full view of the sea. To the S.E. was a large island, probably Julia Percy, and away to the S.W, I thought I could distinguish some rocks at the extremity of the land.

The road led along the top of this ridge for seven or eight miles. On both sides of it were low marshy plains; the one on the right being between the ridge and another line of hills, that on the left being between it and the sandy sea bank. The ridge gradually became flush with the plain and then I left it and crossed over to my left and got on to a track at the base of the sand hummocks. I found this too heavy walking, so I cut over on to the beach. The tide was out and the sand was hard, consequently I rattled along for a long time. Wondering why I saw no signs of the Fitzroy river, I crossed the sea ridge once more and again got on to the track. This I followed until I came to the Fitzroy.

The river seemed to me to be a narrow arm of the sea running parallel to the beach on the sea side of the hummocks. The other bank was pure white sand with only one or two trees on it. Crossing a small tributary I turned up inland to make enquiries at a house I saw. Having received directions I started away at 7 pm. for the only house of accommodation near, distant four miles off.

Marcus Clarke, the Australian novelist, who wrote the preface to *Knocking About in New Zealand* by Charles M Money (1871) (Tom Thompson Collection).

A Glimpse of Port Fairy and the River Moyne.

I fell in with the main road and telegraph line just as it was getting dark. In this walk I disturbed ten or twelve kangaroos. Though quite dark I managed to make my way to the house mentioned, owned by one Brownlaw. The people were the most sour tempered wrangling lot I have ever seen. The room I was put in had for walls thin wooden partitions, so that I could hear everything going on.

In the middle of the night I was awakened by somebody driving furiously up to the house, shouting out 'House there! House; well you are a fine lot of people', and the latter he kept repeating. Mrs. Brownlaw yells out: 'What the devil do you want?'. 'Some matches' was the reply. But for this, and another time when the owner had some gun practice at a native cat and opossum in a tree quite close, I slept well.

Tuesday January 20th.

After a good breakfast I left about 7 p.m.

My walk yesterday was thirty-one miles. The day promised to be a regular scorcher. Somehow or other I didn't feel at all in good trim and every few minutes I had to lay down and rest. The country was well timbered and pretty. About two and a half miles from Brownlaws; you come to the Darrow, a swift beautiful clear stream which glides along perfectly noiselessly. The banks are low and covered with nettles. I had a delightful walk and a drink, crossed the wooden bridge and shortly afterwards came to another bridge. This was over a chain of waterholes which form the beginning of the Fitzroy river. The last post town was Tyrendarra. I still walked on though the heat was intense and the hot wind scorching. I called in at a house to see if I could get some fruit and chummed in with the owner, an old digger, Frederick Saunders. He came to Portland forty three years ago, so he says, and shortly afterwards came to his present habitation. He has seen some stirring life on the diggings and has a vivid recollection of it. He had no fruit, but directed me to try across the road at another house. Here I bought seven and a half pounds of apricots and had a good feed.

I had still fourteen miles to go, so I started away again about 3 o'clock. Bush fires were all about up in the ranges, travelling fast towards me. The smoke spoilt the view. The road took me straight to where I could get a view of the sea and then turned away to the right parallel with the coast. For four miles now the country was perfectly flat and there was not a tree under which I could get shelter nearer than the ranges on my right.

The Surrey is a river nine miles from Portland and has a most extra- ordinary course. From the bridge it was seen to flow first almost due east, then to turn sharp round and flow almost west, till it was brought up on the beach by a sandbar. The water is salt and the banks are low and marshy. Just near the bridge and close to the water's edge there is a spring of splendid water.

The telegraph line now stretched away in a spectral ridge over the white sand. I took the beach and kept it without intermission for seven miles. The banks were still low, but in front of me, where I thought Portland was, the hills heightened and I saw houses on the top. Lawrence Rocks were distinctly visible.

It was now getting quite dark as I left the beach and went on to the road. Walking was very tiring, but I had to keep on as it was getting very dark. I came to two or three water courses and had to go round them. I completely lost sight of the road and had to keep alongside the telegraph line. This shortly went up a high hill and then kept along the top quite close to the edge. It was now pitch dark and I was blundering in all directions. Fancying I could see a high fence on my right, I went up with the intention of sleeping under the lee of it. It was the cemetery, so I didn't wait.

I wasn't long now getting on to the main road and as it was very late hurried on like the mischief. After walking two miles I got into Portland and stopped at the first hotel I met. I was too tired to eat anything, so asked for my room. Some distance had to be gone over uncarpeted stairs arid balcony till I got to it. The flies were frightful, the room smelt horribly. I therefore opened the window as high as it would go and jumped into one of the beds. There were two others in the room. The fleas were in countless numbers. In the morning I wasn't called till breakfast was finished, so all I got was some cold fish recooked, old bread and rancid butter. My bill came to two shillings and six pence. Perhaps it will be as well to remember the name of the house of dirt. It was the 'Lamb' hotel owned by S. McConachy, late of Geelong who told me he was a friend of my father's.

I strolled about before leaving. Portland is a flourishing place and is connected by railway with Melbourne. The bay especially is very fine and there is a long new wharf situated between the old wharf and a tumbledown bathing house.

On the Point to the left is a wreck that has been there since long before the first white man settled in Portland. On the point to the right is the flagstaff and lighthouse. The best hotels are Mac's fronting the bay Paramon's also fronting the bay and late residence of Mr. Henty and the London hotel. While on the wharf, the S.S. *Victoria* called in on her way to Adelaide. The boats are wretched looking things, but well enough adapted for all the fishing there is. I saw Tom Mad [sir Mud] riding and beckoned to him, but he was evidently frightened to come up and speak. I failed again to get a map and after sending away a couple of postcards, one to Mother, the other to Stewart McArthur, started for Bridgewater, a place I had been strongly recommended to go to by Mrs. Begg, who had given me a letter of introduction to a man there.

The day was in every way a contrast to yesterday. Though it didn't rain, it had every appearance of being about to do so. To get to Bridgewater you have to follow the Mt Gambier road for five and a half miles and then turn away to the left. The customary Australian bush scenery is met with and water can be procured at a swamp on the road. After turning off from the main road the track becomes one of very heavy sand, which of course adds proportionately to the fatigue of walking. The road has many branches but they all lead back again. One stream of running water is crossed by a bridge and soon after you come within sight of the sea cliffs and keep within sight henceforth.

The country as you go on becomes more open and a great part of it is under cultivation. After passing several houses you come on to the top of a hill from where you can see Cape Bridgewater, a comparatively narrow neck of land running out in to the sea. A branch road takes you out on the E. side of this at the foot of a range of hills, quite bare and pigeonholed with rabbit burrows. You cannot see McKinley's house till you come to the end of this road, when you see it on the side of the cape, fronting you with the sea between.

One or two other houses are behind it. I went up to the house and presented my letter from Mrs. Begg. McKinley said he had no room in the house at first but sooo recollected that he could give me a shakedown I was very hungry so had a glorious tea in the kitchen. I was strolling about afterwards and went down on to the rocks, to a hut where I saw some men. These are fishermen engaged in pursuit of Haddock or Trevalla. There are eighteen in all; their boats are wretched little things and they are not born fishermen at all, being sons of farmers.

Afterwards I was accosted by a military looking fellow, who asked me one or two questions. I told him who I was and what I was travelling for. He immediately became very friendly and without the slightest reserve told me that he was the State School teacher and had done trips similar to mine for many years in New Zealand. He introduced me to a squatter from the Wimmera stopping here, a Mr. Wettenhall. 'This is Mr. Morrison who, to my mind, is doing a very plucky thing. He has walked all the way from Queenscliff round the coast and intends to go on to Adelaide. What makes it all the more plucky is that he is seventeen years of age and has never done anything like it before.'

Mr. Wettenhall has his wife and seven children down also and the other visitors are a Mr. Thomson, a miserable, syphilitic looking storekeeper from Hamilton, his wife and three children, who told me his brother used to come to the College.

Mr. Charles L. Money, the schoolmaster, is an extraordinary man. In appearance he is five feet eleven inches high, broad shouldered and remarkably well made. He has fair hair, blue eyes, an energetic nose and determined mouth. He is of a very impetuous disposition, very impatient of rebuke. He is forty years of age, but being so fashionably dressed and wearing such a handsome moustache easily might be mistaken for twenty-five. The family is a very good one. His father was in the army and his cousin Walter L. Money has been distinguishing himself in the Afghan War. Mr. Money was educated at Eton and then entered the army. He was a soldier for three years in India, if I remember in the 97th. He has been in Alexandria

Mr. Money came out to New Zealand many years ago. He was the first white man on the West coast and his explorations and adventures were narrated by him in a book called *Knocking About in New Zealand*, published by Samuel Mullen (1871), of which five hundred copies were sold. He was a frightful fellow to drink and for five years spent all he had to gratify his passion. As a common carrier deporting a load on his back over the mountains earned three pound a day. He fought during the Maori War and was under fire nine times. He has been several things in Victoria, was at the diggings, was a swagman and at another time was a traveller for a photographer. Nine years ago he received a situation at the G.G.S. He got drunk and was dismissed. He has been a tee-totaller since, is now earning a one hundred pound a year as a State School teacher and is engaged to be married to a girl who subscribes herself in her letters 'Your loving little kitten.'

Notwithstanding Mr. McKinley professed his inability to make me comfortable, I could not have been more so. In the morning before breakfast we men had a bathe in the sea. The breakers were glorious and it was very enjoyable. Cape Bridgewater is the western extremity of a deep bay, the cape opposite being Cape Nelson. McKinley's house is situated on the slope of this high headland, looking towards Cape Nelson. Below is a rocky beach, but at the head of the bay is a long strip of beautiful sand. The bay is the finest I have ever seen. It is protected by high hills, the majority of which were covered with the usual vegetation seen near the sea -- but there is one strip about a mile long on the E. side of the bay of perfectly white sand mountains.

In the morning I went with Wettenhall and Thomson, taking McKinley as guide, to see some fine caves at the end of the cape. The scenery about is fine and rugged. The first cave is entered by an opening to get to which you have to scramble up a place six feet high and as steep as the side of a house. It is about twenty or thirty yards long, of limestone formation, and therefore ornamented with the usual stalactites. The other cave is like a huge and lofty hall and does not run in very far.

McKinley gave us a Gaelic song in the latter and it was a truthful mixture of the sublime and the ridiculous.

In the afternoon I went much further round the coast to see some blowholes. Nothing I have seen anywhere round the coast can be even compared with the sublime scenery thereof. It was a calm day when I saw it, yet often when the waves struck the rocks they would send up a cloud of spray far above our heads and we were sitting eighty feet above the water on a ledge of rock. The cliffs here are of a dark blue colour, in formation and general appearance somewhat like the pictures of the Giants' Causeway. On a rough day you cannot come near the top of the cliffs at all or you would be wet through instantly.

We saw two blowholes. Immediately after a wave thunders up against the rocks a huge puff of steam, smoke or water shoots out of these holes with a noise like a cannon. The rougher the weather, the louder the explosion The waves are sublime they are magnificent. By Jerusalem I wish I could describe them. I know I could have looked at them for hours without getting tired.

Mr. Money can't go near the edge of the cliffs, as he is seized with an irresistible desire to throw himself in and several times it has been all he could do to prevent himself.

Mr. McKinley certainly feeds you well. His wife is an old, sunken woman and everlasting talker and wears spectacles.

Friday January 23rd.

Next day, Friday, I asked her how much there was to pay. 'Would a shilling a meal be too much, Sir?' Only seven shillings.

I left about 9.30 and was accompanied by Mr. Wettenhall, Mr. Thomson and McKinley. We were bound for some lakes near the coast on the western side of Cape Bridgewater. A walk of six miles over hills and sand brought us to them. The rabbits were about in swarms. Some curious caves on the side of a hill are worth seeing. Though there were several lakes when we saw them, I expect they are all united in winter.

We had dinner with an old Scotch body from Wigtonshire. From her house you get a fine view of the sea. The gentlemen then left for home and I started onwards. I went straight up across Mr. Thomson's ground till I struck the road which would take me to the main road. I took a wrong turning to the left, however, and thus lost a mile. Mr. Morse put me right. I again got on to the road. This led past a school house along near the sea coast for four miles. A wire fence abruptly stopped me, but seeing a house in the distance, I crossed over to it, getting on to a road doing so. While walking along I was accosted by a man in a field with 'Good day, mate. Can you do binding?' I went up to him and he tried to persuade me to stop and do some binding for the next two days. I, of course, regretted that I hadn't time. Having received directions to the nearest house of accommodation, kept by one Hedditch, I started. The road is heavy and much used by carts, so there is no mistaking it. When you come to where it branches you must take the one to the right, the left one being the old coast road to the Punt.

After a walk of four miles through thickly timbered country I came out on to the Telegraph line and main road between Portland and the Punt at the eighteenth milestone from Portland. Hedditch's house is at the twenty fourth milestone and when I got there it was quite dark. The country abounds with kangaroos; I must have disturbed fifty or sixty. I also saw twelve cockatoos, white ones, flying overhead.

As it was so late and I had been told Hedditch's was at the nine- teen milestone, I began to fear that I. had missed it. I had almost made up my mind to camp when I heard the barking of dogs. Knowing that they must be at some house, I kept on and soon had the satisfaction of making out the outline of a house on a rise to my left.

I didn't feel at all well today. Some crayfish which I took last night disagreeing with me. I had as good a bed as anyone could wish for and a fine breakfast. I left about 11 o'clock feeling very weak. The road is a single broad wagon track of heavy sand, very heavy walking. Thickly timbered country and I saw many kangaroos.

Saturday January 24th.

Hedditch's house is twenty-four miles from Portland and three miles further on is a sly grog accommodation house owned by one Johnstone. I got a glass of brandy here which did me good. Through his paddock runs a stream of beautiful water.

About thirty-five miles from Portland, a short distance off the main road on the left, is a spring of water which tasted very much of the swamp. I took a billy full of it with me, but getting tired of carrying it, threw it away. Shortly afterwards I met a fellow traveller bound for Johnstone's He was very thirsty, but I couldn't relieve him.

The country gradually becomes more open and there are farm houses about. I killed a thin little snake lying in the middle of the road. From what I have learned since I think it must have been a whip snake. Kangaroos are very plentiful. I also saw some large birds, black with apparently a hood on, and I believe they were black cockatoos.

The Glenelg is forty-four miles from Portland and is crossed by a punt. The man that works the punt has been down there thirty years on the 19th February. His name is Brown and for the convenience of visitors he has erected a large white stone house. I went to bed immediately on getting there and in the morning I had breakfast inside. Stopping here are some Casterton residents. One, a Mr. Curtis, a fat common-looking man with a big paunch, whiskers on his chin and wore spectacles. He had a slight cast in his eyes. Another was a fine tall man with a red moustache and whiskers down the side of his face. His chin was shaved. Another was an oldish man, a shopkeeper I should say, though apparently respectable.

I left about 11.20 a.m. The Glenelg is a beautiful river, very broad and deep. In the distance about a mile away I could see the beach and people walking on it. The banks are high, especially on the western side. I was told there is some very fine scenery high up the river.

I have now walked from Queenscliff to the Punt (below), a distance of three hundred and twenty-nine miles and I have resolved to go on to Adelaide.

The road from the Glenelg to Mt. Gambier is across hills, low ones, mostly covered with ferns. There is a telegraph line all the way and a well defined road. You pass on the road the spot where a German named - shot a bailiff. He was the first of the two criminals who have been executed in the Mount. Before getting into the town I passed many houses, all with flourishing fields attached to them. The township of Gambier lies on the north east side of Mount Gambier. This mount has the appearance of a cone that has melted away at the top and run down the sides, whereas Mount Schanck which you see away to your left, seems to have had its top sawn off.

The town is very flourishing and when I got in just after Church the streets were crowded. I asked someone to direct me to the best house to stop at. He showed me the way to a boarding house kept by a Mrs Barratt, called Barratt's Temperance Hotel. I gave the girl that came to the door a severe fright and then sat down to tea in a dirty little room with three doors leading into it: one to the bar where men were drinking, smoking and laughing; another to the kitchen where lascivious men were smoking and spitting and drinking; and another to a room where women were eating and giggling. I found that the room in which I was to sleep was also occupied by five other men, so I was in doubts whether to stay, but when I heard a man sick just overhead and the servants addressing swagmen as Sir, my mind was speedily made up. I first went to a fashionable hotel and in the most freezingly polite manner was informed by a short snobbish man with slopey shoulders, loud dress and bookmaker tout ensemble that he would be only too delighted to allow the boots to show me an hotel better suited for such as me. I meekly asked where. 'There,' was the information, accompanied by a majestic wave of his hand that took in all Mt. Gambier. In the most sarcastic manner this insufferable essence of conceit wished me a cordial goodnight and then went inside, no doubt chuckling in his sleeve at his wit.

At Newton's Hotel I spent a comfortable night and had a good breakfast. I bought some German sausage and bread and then consulted a map in the Mechanics. I find that my shortest way to get to Adelaide is by the old overland route, so today I started for Glencoe, eighteen miles distant. There is a metal road for the first five or six miles, but then it turns away up to the left and you keep straight on. A gate is passed and then you are in Glencoe H.S. For some distance the track is alongside the old telegraph line to Penola. A spring of green water is met with. Scenery here dead trees, ferns, telegraph poles and crows. Further on, before coming into the open, in which is the homestead, the scenery is convalescent stringybark trees, grass trees, tree ferns and kangaroos with a heavy sandy road to deaden it and a swamp or two for variety.

The homestead consists of two very large, long two-storied buildings like barracks, several outhouses and two large woolsheds like churches. I did not intend to stop, but found I had to. The men said I ought not to go on but should stay with them. See us at tea: fifteen or eighteen men with a pannikin of sweet tea and no milk, a tin platter knife and fork. Cabbage is put on the table and each one helps himself largely. There are no potatoes. Haricot follows and is hungrily partaken of by the men.

The station belongs to the family of Leake in Tasmania and is rented by the brothers Lindsay. Stopping here on a visit was Alan Skinner. In the evening the men had a dance in a large room containing ten or twelve berths and then there was throwing of the dice for matches in the kitchen. I slept in a box formerly used for horse feed in a small room in a stable. In the next room was a race horse. My blanket was an old horse rug and the fleas were strong.

Next morning I had an early breakfast and then started for Mt. Graham. I was shown a track which took me to a boundary rider's hut 1½ miles from the homestead. Tho man in it told me that after passing through a gate I would come to two roads and I was to take the one to the left. The water about here is that very hard spring limestone water and today I suffered much from diarrhoea. I went through the gate but could discern no track turning to the left, so kept straight on. The track was very indistinct, but I managed to find my way across a long plain, mostly dead timber, with a green stringybark every here and there. The road gradually turned over an incline to the right, in the very direction I wished it and very shortly afterwards I came to a fence and a white gate, such as I had been informed I would meet with two miles from the boundary rider's hut.

I am now out of Glencoe station and in the forest. The trees are very fine, but the walking is heavy. Ferns are, of course, the only grass.

The road turns slightly to the left along the edge of a swamp. As I am wearily toiling along four majestic emus cross the path just in front. The one leading is an immense big fellow and towers above his three companions. The direction I am going is exactly at right angles to the nearest way to Mr. Hay's, but a large swamp lies between, which cannot be crossed.

After walking five miles I come upon four small huts and a tent at the head of the swamp and at the foot of a hill, wooded and covered with ferns. This is Mount Burr. I go to one of the houses and ask the woman if I may sit down as it is fearfully hot and I don't feel at all well. She tells me to make myself comfortable and sets some dinner before me. Her husband is away, but her next door neighbour is splitting wood and will be home to dinner. His name is Deane and he used to work for Dr. Curdie. He was the first one to learn of the wreck of the Maria Gabriel and gave the first intelligence of it. This vessel, it will be remembered, struck near Moonlight Head and was immediately forsaken by the crew. These men made their way along the cliffs to Cape Otway. They were three days in doing it and when they arrived they were in a frightful state. I'm not sure if some of them did not die on the road. Strangely enough the vessel, when out at sea, had picked up a canoe of South Sea Islanders which had drifted away from land. On landing these men went away by themselves and were found dead within a mile of the wreck. Dr. Curdie bought the wreck and did well out of it, as its cargo was a valuable one of tea. Deane and another man had to protect the cargo from the crowds of loafers that had rushed, as men always do, to the place with the hope of gain. The former sold the ship's bell to a man for one pound. The buyer was carrying his purchase up the cliffs when he met Dr. Curdie who directed him where to leave it. He and his mate made thirty pounds each.

As I have nine miles to go, I say goodbye to Deane about 3 o'clock as soon as he has shown me the track. The road is still very heavy sand through a stringybark forest and does not improve till I come to a fence newly erected. For a short distance it is across a hard dry swamp, but then it gradually gets as bad as ever. Walking is hot and the heat of the sand nearly burns my soles off. Scenery never changes till I go through a gate. Hills are all about, covered with ferns near me, but the ones some distance back are bare.

Wreck Bay, Moonlight Head.

The road now divides into two. I luckily take the one to the right as it seems the best beaten. I was walking now quite in the open, round the sides of gentle slopes. I had been told that when I came to where someone was buried I was to look straight ahead and I should see an old chimney marking the spot where once a settler had his home; Mt. Graham would be in front of me and Mr. Hay's house on the other side. Well here was the tomb on the left and the chimney on the right. I went up to the tomb. It was a stone slab enclosed with a high stone railing, as long ago as 1850, to a boy of sixteen.

    I followed the road and meeting a bullock driver I learn that I am well on my way to Millicent. By turning north and following the east foot of the hill I strike the road which takes me to the house. Nearby were a number of men driving sheep. One of them points out Mr. Hay to me and I go up to him and tell my name and the object of my walk. He smiled incredulously when I told him I was a son of George Morrison, but nevertheless told me I should get what I wanted from the woman in the kitchen.

    I had tea with the men and afterwards was summoned into the presence of Mr. Hay who apologised for keeping me in the kitchen. Another young fellow, Willie Wells, lives with him. I drank too much whiskey, got damned well screwed and during the night nearly spewed my guts out

Wednesday January 28th.

Up at daybreak and washed up everything. I resolved to take a spell today and in the morning wrote to Mama. I told her I was well into South Australia and that I had resolved to walk to Adelaide, that I would be home in three or four weeks, but on no account to be anxious.

The day was most fearfully hot so I didn't go out till evening, when took a gun to try and get a kangaroo. Numbers were seen and I had three or four shots, but unsuccessful. Crossing the fence to get on yesterday's track, I annihilated one.

After tea, it being full moon, Willie and I went out shooting again, but it was too cloudy to take aim with any accuracy, so we go home.

Mr. Hay is a short rough-looking man, as thin as a crow, with a tremendous lot of bushy hair and whiskers. He is a brother of Mrs. Hensley and Miss MacDonald and partner of Tom Guthrie.

Thursday January 29th.

It was even hotter than yesterday and at any rate far too hot to walk. Mrs. Pearson washed all my things. The station is gradually being eaten up by selectors. The house is very large and mostly unfurnished. After dinner I went for a walk on to the top of Mt. Graham. From there you can see one of the finest views in South Australia. Looking south you see Lake Frome at the other side of a low range of hills. To the S.W. four miles distant, is Mt. Muirhead and away to the W. you can just distinguish the white sand cliffs. The range of hills from Mt. Burr to Mt. Graham is easily made out. Turning round you see the Reedy Creek Swamp stretching for miles and miles in a N.W. direction. To the N.E. is a pretty lake and the rest of the picture is taken up with hills, conspicuous among which are the Woakewine Range away to the W.N.W. The house is on the northern slope of Mt. Graham and in the plain at its feet lies the Reedy Creek and near it are the stock yards.

On my way up the Mount I had shot a large brush kangaroo and it struck me that I might get one or two by watching for them from a tree. Accordingly I, with much labour, hauled gun and self up a stringybark, sat down on a thin rough limb and waited. I hadn't been there five minutes before a kangaroo came and squatted underneath. I was so overjoyed that I forgot to fire and while manoeuvring to get aim, the animal hopped quietly off. I sat for two hours longer in agony, but nothing appeared. I was just getting ready to descend when one, out of pity for me, came too close and paid the penalty.

The water about here is excellent and near the old chimney mentioned before are some celebrated caves which contain water as cold as ice and clear as crystal.

Friday January 30th.

It was again hot. I was accompanied for a couple of miles by Boyle, a horsebreaker, who put me on the road and then left me. I had a fence on my right hand side all the way. At one place I pass a splendid reedy lake swarming with ducks. On the roadside were magnificent thick-barked blue gums and blackwoods. I meet a man on horseback and he gives me further directions. A fire has been here and burnt down a mile or two of the fence, but still the road is perfectly distinct. I am surprised when it turns away almost at right angles; as the road turns away, of course I do too. Shortly I come into the open, a large plain of that coarse bushy grass, with a heavy sandy road. I met two fellow travellers who tell me it is nine miles to Gillup, my destination, where they sundowned last night The road turns again and runs due north. You pass through a beautiful grassy sward, shaded by a few immense blue gums with their delightfully refreshing green foliage. To add to the attractiveness of the picture an emu is quietly stalking across it and two or three kangaroos, disturbed in their afternoon siesta, are timidly hopping into the scrub. Leaving this pretty spot the whole plain on your right, dotted with honeysuckles, appears to get more marsh-like and as you go on gradually inclining to the N.W. you see that it is a dry swamp. The track is on the edge of this and unmistakable as you cannot turn in to the left owing to the dense scrub of ferns and dry wattles, she- oaks and honeysuckles. On a pretty little sheet of water near the road, surrounded with reeds, three swans are majestically swimming and several blue cranes, startled in their fishing, are just getting ready to fly off.

I kept along like this at the edge of the Reedy Creek, which I afterwards learnt was the name of the swamp, till I got to the house wanted a few yards off from the road. The gentleman to whom I had the letter of introduction, the manager, Mr. McDonald has lately created a lot of amusement in matrimonial circles. He got engaged to a girl and jilted her. She brought a breach of promise action against him and obtained three hundred and fifty pounds damages. Her excuse for the engagement was that she could never be afraid of being jealous, he was so ugly. In manner I found him a very kindhearted Scotchman. He seems to be about fifty years of age and has a genial nice face. The overseer, Mr. McKeand, is a fine big Irishman. The room I had was very large and so was the bed and the latter appeared to be very clean. During the night I positively suffered agonies from the attacks of bugs. I felt perfectly mad from the irritation and my back and arms from vicious scratching are one mass of lumps.

Saturday January 31st.

My walk yesterday had been eighteen miles and today I started for Foster's, seventeen miles distant. It was most fearfully hot. About half a mile from the house you cross the Penola Road, known from there being an old public house on it to your left and from the bridge where it crosses the Reedy Creek, now dry.

My directions were 'Keep along the edge of the swamp. You will pass through three gates. Two miles beyond the third you will see a wagon road turning to your left into the bush. Follow it and it will take you to Pearson's. The heat was very trying and the atmosphere close because of my proximity to the swamp. This so-called swamp is more a rush-covered plain. I saw no water in it, but in winter time there is a sluggish flowing stream extending fifty or so miles in length and of an average breadth of two or three miles. I had been told that I would see a great many emus about, but up till now I had only seen five today. However, I saw one running in a bare patch one great big fellow followed by seven little ones. I also met today, two native companions, the first wild ones I had ever seen.

The road which turns up into the bush doesn't do so at a very abrupt angle and might easily be passed by a traveller not keeping a careful look out Once well in the bush it turns gradually to the left until you come to a nice stone wall enclosing a garden. The scenery is the common Australian bush scenery. It was in the very heat of the day that

I went up to the house and I was perspiring from every pore. The distance from Gillup to the turn-off is nine miles and from there to the house three more.

I find that the property belongs to Mrs. Crowe and is managed by her brother, a Mr. Ryan, a long black-haired Irishman. He says that I had better stop with him as Mr. Foster isn't very hospitable to strangers. Accordingly I resolve to do so. In the afternoon there comes across on a visit a Mr. Watson who comes from within a mile or two of Edirikillis. He has heard of my father. The house is as usual, a very large one with a large orchard. The apple trees are the most prolific I have ever seen.

Sunday February 1st.

It was one of the hottest days man ever did work on. I was up very late and so didn't leave Reedy Creek station till near ten o'clock. I was put on the track to Foster's and was painfully toiling on there in a fearfully hot frame of mind and body, with a terrific sun shining down from a cloudless sky on my devoted head. I had gone about a mile when I heard a horseman approaching. It was Mr. Watson wanting to know if I would come across to his place and spend the day there and then tomorrow I could go to a Mr. McBain's at Mt. Benson's, another old Morayshire man, and walk into Kingston next day.

Though it would take me a day longer than my present route and was twenty-five miles further, I didn't need much pressing to turn back. I like to take a spell if possible on Sunday and another thing the route he mentioned would take me nearer the coast. Accordingly I turned back and after a walk of four miles got to his nice little house, was warmly welcomed by his wife and spent a pleasant day. Mrs. Watson was a Mis McGinis and to her brother at Grower I have a letter of introduction from Mr. Hay. In the evening we went after kangaroos but none were got. There is a family of seven and the governess, Miss McDonald, used to be with the Rev. Mr. Turnbull. Mr. Watson is a short, bright-eyed, dark-whiskered man and was a schoolmaster when he picked up an heiress.

Early on Monday, which gave promise of being again very

hot, was put on the track. The land all about here is covered in winter time for miles with water. After passing through a gate six miles from Konetta, you meet a road crossing it at right angles, but not very well beaten. This runs between a station on Lake Hawdon and the Penola Road.

Water can be got anywhere just by digging for it. There is one water hole, but the water is too dirty to drink. In front you see the Stonehut Ranges, a continuation of the Woakewine Ranges and on getting nearer you find a swamp on your right hand side. This is Lake Hawdon Swamp and Is one of the largest in South Australia. When at the base of the hills you see across this dreary plain of rushes, about two miles off, a very large stone house with a smaller one also of stone to the left of it. The telegraph line runs close beside the house. Though I had been distinctly told no one lived there, I resolved to go across and see if I could get a drink. At the double gate where the road I am on joins the metal road between Penola and Robe, a tent is pitched, but no one is inside it. I have since learnt that a sprIng of beautifully cold water is quite close to it. I followed the metal road along till I came to the twelve mile post when, instead of going straight away over the ranges, I laid down my knapsack and turned up to the right beside the telegraph along an old wagon path and after a walk of a mile came to a house. The first one was unoccupied but the large one, In my great joy, had inhabitants.

It was now 10.30 a.m. and I had come twelve miles. I rested. The woman was a little old English body, a native of Bury Street. Edmunds on of an old Shropshire family, a distant connection of John Bright. She is engaged in the occupation of making mats and rugs etc., out of skins of native game shot by her son or by her husband. She has exhibited with credit at the Philadelphia, Vienna and other exhibitions. She gave me my dinner and would charge nothing for it.

The son told me that at the nine mile post I should see a sheep yard and from it I could see the Springs, a favourite picnic place of the Robe people on account of the beautiful water. From where I was I could have taken a short cut, but I had to go back for my knapsack and then it was shorter to go by the main road. From the top of the hill you get a view of what seems at first sight to be an arm of the sea, but on getting round further you see that it is a lake. This is Lake Eliza, some miles in length and some miles in breadth, with low marshy banks, though protected by a chain of hills. Just below where I stand there is a farmhouse and newly mown paddock, but all the rest of the country seems too poor to have population.

When I came to the ninth mile post and the old sheep yard, I look about but can find no water. It was very tantalizing to be, as I knew I was, so near without being able to have a drink. I have since learnt that the springs are one hundred or one hundred and fifty yards from the sheep yard on the other side of the road. In a couple of miles I come to a large house about half a mile off the road. This is Richmond Park belonging to Thomas Stockdale. It was 4.30 and by the road still fourteen miles further to Mr. McBain's at Mt. Benson. I asked if there were not a short cut and was told that I could get to Martin's eight miles off by a track and from there could get shown the way to McBain's about a mile further on.

My directions were these, and whether they were given in ignorance or with an intention to lead me astray, I do not know. 'You are to follow this track (barely distinguishable) till you come to a metal road to Narracoorte. Keep the road until you see a track turning away at right angles. Follow that for two miles and you will come a gate. Two miles further on a waterhole will be right in your path. From there you will be able to see a stone wall which is got through by a gate. Shortly afterwards you will come to the stock yard on top of a hill, from which a track will take you to Martin's. There are several old houses, but Martin's is the first on the left.'

Accordingly, on getting to the metal road I was taken across the range once more and near the foot of it I saw a track turning away to the left, but not by any means at right angles. I followed it, however, and was brought out into the open at the edge of Lake Hawdon Swamp. The track followed along the foot of a range of hills branching out in all directions and several times passed over the neck between the main range and an out- lying hill. On one of these I came to a gate and to my right was a yard of high post and rail fences. I expect that was the sheep yard. About four miles further on I pass one or two deserted huts. Out of curiosity I turned up a track here and found it led to a muddy waterhole. Soon afterwards I came to a wire fence running across the wide plain and this joins onto a stone wall. After getting through the second stone wall I still have the ranges of hills on my left, till turning round a corner I see a house. I found it was deserted and the well dry. I would have camped here only I was so thirsty that I thought I would go on a little further and see if I could come to another house. A mile or two further along a heavy road I had the satisfaction of seeing a large white house on the side of the hills overlooking the dreary yellow swamp. A haystack was in an enclosure in front, so I had no doubt about the house being uninhabited.

The proprietor was Mrs. Martin. She told me that she was a widow, that it was two miles to Mr. McBain's and most likely that he wasn't at home, so I had better stop with her. The suggestion was acted on as I was tired after my walk of thirty miles on such a hot day. She has two daughters and two sons in the house and they are in very comfortable circumstances. They have only been thirteen years in the Colony and come from Devonshire.

Tuesday February 3rd.

It was with one exception, the hottest day I ever walked on. I got away about 9 o'clock to walk the seventeen miles into Kingston. On getting on the top of the hill that protected the house, I could see the telegraph line right below me which was there to show me the way into Kingston. I pass a school house and several other houses, and for a good long way there is a wire fence on both sides of the road. This stops and then the scenery became positively painful to look at. A bright blue sky without a cloud to temper the heat of the sun; a heavy road of brown sand; withered honeysuckles; the whole country recently swept by fire and the cursed black telegraph poles. I tried to while away the time by counting the poles, but that wouldn't do. I lie down under a honeysuckle and proceed to write up my diary (a fortnight in arrears), but it was too hot to do even that. In despair I jump up and resolve not to stop till I come to a house. For five miles I didn't see a blade of grass, but then I came in sight of a nice paddock, with a long grassy swamp stretching away in the direction of the poles. A house, of course, is near. The first exclamation of the owner is 'What the devil don't you cover your arms for? (For the last day or two I had been wearing only a sleeveless jersey). You take my word for it, if you don't take care you'll have to spend a holiday in thehospital.'

The speaker is a pretty tall dark man, apparently with a temper of his own and very bitter against the squatters and the South Australian Government. He had gone on a walk to see about taking up a selection near Apollo Bay, but hearing of a great fire which was raging about here, he had to hurry back. This and the fact that for the last eight days he hasn't been out of doors because of the heat, had no doubt put him in a bad humour.

His name is Harry Lush, a quondam sailor, but now a successful tanner and preparer and worker up of native skins. He sailed in a schooner with an old Captain Ennis who was deaf as a post and no wonder. He went in a schooner with a number of men on a pearl cruise in the South Sea Islands. The majority of the hands had occasion to leave the vessel, leaving Ennis with three other men in charge. The men were no sooner out of sight when the schooner was attacked by South Sea lslanders. Such numbers swarmed on deck as to drive the white men to seek refuge below. The fight raged, countless blacks slain, but Ennis' mates were killed and he alone remained. He made up his mind that he had to die, so going to the magazine he applied a lighted match to the powder. The top of the vessel blew off with a fearful roar, carrying the blacks into eternity (Lush says that for all he knows they may be sailing about there yet). When the men returned they found nothing but the blackened hull. Ennis was found up the for'ard, a shapeless mass. By the force of the explosion he had been driven through two oaken hogsheads with no greater permanent injury than the loss of hearing.

He showed me some shells got close to the surface and also a magnificent tiger sealskin which he is now tanning. For size and beauty it excels anything ever seen. It is thirteen feet in length by an average width of five feet. Down the centre - the back - it is of a rich brown colour merging into a beautiful metallic gold on either side. The time I spent with Lush during the heat of the day was most interesting. I took a great fancy to him and gave him a lot of useful information about the coast. His wife was very kind and wanted me to spend the day and night.

You take up the telegraph line again at his tannery and before coming to any timber it crosses a wide marshy plain, now perfectly dry, but covered to a depth of two or three feet with water in winter time. After passing through the belt of timber you again come into a plain of long grass, this time particularly large and extending as far as you can see. The sea cliffs are visible on your left. The telegraph comes out on the main road near the fifth mile post from Kingston and it is an uninteresting walk to the township. Where there wasn't the marshy plain, you had instead these grassy hills ridging from the road. About a mile from Kingston you cross by a bridge an apology for a creek and near it on the left hand side is a nice cemetery.

The township is very straggled and seemed to be of recent date. saw here two things which I hadn't seen for some time: the sea and the railway station. The former not since leaving the Punt, the latter not since I had left Queenscliff. I made my way to Clink's Kingston Arms Hotel, not at all a nice place. After tea I took a stroll about, bought a waterbag for three shillings and went down onto the beach. There is a magnificent jetty nearly three quarters of a mile long and twelve feet broad. It had come on quite cold and was so dark that I could hardly see anything.

My eighteenth birthday was Wednesday, February 4th, 1880. had an early though not a very enjoyable breakfast and started away for my long looked for trip down the Coorong to Meningie. My bill was six shillings and I wouldn't advise any person to stop there.

The first mile post I came to showed that it is one hundred and twenty miles to Wellington where I go to after leaving Meningie. You cross the small river Maria and then the road leads below the sand hummocks, with a long stretch of grassy flats on your right. The scenery never varies. I spent the first night at Mrs. Roberts at the sixteenth mile-post.

The next day was still nice and cool. The grassy flats gradually merged into chains of white lakes, perfectly dry, in some places covered with low stunted bushes. At the other side was seen what looked like a flat of ti-tree and a range of hills was in the distance. The road I was on, instead of keeping at the base of the sand cliff, kept over grassy plains, while the sand cliffs retreated to the left and bare, grassy hills rose between. Every now and then, however, an outlying sand range came across the path and you had to go round it. The telegraph line kept all the way. The road is a good one and in places, where it led close to or crossed beside the pipeclay, was made. Just before getting to Coolatoo you pass through some miles of the same grassy flats.

Mr. Robson of the hotel made me very comfortable. He told me that the beautiful green trees at the other side of the pipeclay and between it and the range of hills is the celebrated Mallee. The coach calls here to enable the parson to get some tea. When I got to the hotel Mr. Sinclair, the clergyman, of Kingston was christening Mr. Robson's youngest son.

Saturday the 6th.

It was also hot. About ten miles before getting to Coolatoo some men were putting up coach stables. I left about 10.30. After six miles you come to Mr. Gait's out-station Cantara, where I got some water. The road up till now had been on the west side of the pipeclay, but now it gradually worked across and after a mile or two of walking in the pipeclay itself took you to a sandy road on the other side. In a short time you came to some more coach stables at Chinamens' Wells. The water here is very nice, I didn't rest here as it was 3 p.m. and I had eleven miles further to go, Chinamons' Wells being five miles from Cantara.

The road then takes you on to the pipeclay and for eight miles there is delightful walking, though the glare is rather trying to the eyes. In the distance you think of course you see water, but don't come to any for five miles and it is far out in the centre of the pipeclay. Coorong, for such we must now call the pipeclay - is a term only applicable to that portion under water, so its dimensions in winter are not to be compared with it in summer. The Coorong extends at least twenty or twenty-five miles further up than this. On the right of me there are low sandy hummocks, but at the other side, two or three miles off, you see a huge dreary chain of sea cliffs, some of the hills being perfectly white sand. The coach road then keeps along the E. shore for eight miles, when it becomes too rocky, so strikes inland a little. Then by a made portion turns round a rather large hill and shortly afterwards strikes inland for good. You pass a small lake of pipeclay, then turn round another similar lake.

The beautiful mallee bush is here first met with by the traveller, though it has been within sight for miles and miles. It was quite different from anything I expected. I always fancied that the mallee was a short dry looking conglomeration of brown twigs, a dead she-oak on a small scale. Stead of that it is a beautiful bright green foliaged shrub with a leaf like the gum and a very sweet smell.

The road brings you out on to a large tract of pipeclay. On the hill opposite you see a house Crossing the pipeclay and climbing a hill, then turning to the right, you pass over the Salt Creek, an arm of the Coorong, and the house is on the slope to the right. It is the accommodation house of McLeod. From it you get a fine view of the Coorong, with the high sand hummocks on the far side. Grassy slopes in front of the house and mallee bush to the right and left. Below are what look like a pair of beautiful blue lakes - bends in the creek. Turning round you see a hilly extent of country running back for miles and you also get a good view of the Salt Creek.

The house is notorious as once being the residence of the murderer Malachi Martin. The parents of the girl he had as general servant (he was a publican) sent for her to come home to Adelaide. She

had two years wages owing to her and to save this he murdered her, and stuffed her down a wombat hole. The crows betrayed the deed. She was found by the blacks and Malachi expiated his crime. It is suspected that this was not the first murder he committed. A jewellery hawker was missed. Some of his goods were found on Mrs. Martin.

Saturday was so fearfully hot that I thought it advisable to rest during the heat of the day and write up my diary. I am frightfully lax in keeping this. However, at 4.30 p.m. I started. The road is good nearly all the way. Three miles from Salt Creek there is an encampment of the blacks - the first I had ever seen. A mile or two further on there were one or two more. Just before getting to the Mail Stables at Policemens' Point you have a fine stretch of beach to cross. I covered this at a run. Policemens' Point is six miles from McLeod's.

The road now for a bit very sandy. A large and gaudy long American van with four horses is stationary on it. It is filled with a number of young fellows forming some Panorama Company. One was on ahead, walking to reconnoitre. The horses were wretched things.

The next stage is Wood's Wells, a bare peninsula running far into the Coorong. The whole way you are close to the sea and the quantity of teal I saw was simply incredible. For miles along the beach and in the water close to it the teal were settled. They allowed me to get within thirty yards before rising and then they seemed like dense clouds.

The house at Wood's Wells is an old tumbledown stone accommodation place, managed by one Robson and his wife. The former is a fine, handsome fellow and it was most entertaining to talk to him. He was once a sailor and has been nearly all over the world. He has been up the Mediterranean and he quite kindled my enthusiasm by his description of Malta, Cadiz, Carthagena etc.

Sunday gave token of being frightfully hot. I was up early and away by 7 a.m. My road now lay right on the edge of the Coorong. Every few yards there was a mob of six or seven of those lovely mountain ducks. In some bays there would be as many as forty or fifty of them. The teal were also in abundance swimming about further out. The hummocks at the other side of the Coorong are not so high as they have been, but in a few miles they rise up again. The Coorong is studded with beautiful islands, some rocky, but the majority long and narrow and covered with trees. The Coorong is as a rule very shallow and near the coast rocky. Low sharp ledges of rock run out everywhere.

The first house you come to after leaving Wood's Wells is the Mail Stables at Cocoanut Wells, eight miles distant. The man in charge surprised me by telling me that a man can wade across to the other side, a mile and a half off. After leaving the stables your track cuts off an immense peninsula, running far into the Coorong, which must make the channel very narrow, though a man on the banks cannot tell with any certainty. You now lose sight of the Coorong and see an immense tract of pipeclay instead. A hard metal road brings you into McGrath's Flat. This place gets its name from a man McGrath who when driving stock from Sydney to Melbourne was murdered there by the blacks. The hotel is kept by a man McCallum. I spent an hour there and had dinner. McGrath's Flat is four miles from Cocoanut Wells. I left again, though reluctant to do so, as the day was so oppressively hot.

The Coorong is here met with again and on its low banks below the house were three wurleys - blackfellows' camping places. They are made of old sacks slung on sticks and are about the most wretched looking habitations a being could live in. The islands opposite are very pretty, covered with grass and honeysuckles which in the distance give it a very park like appearance.

I had started to walk into Meningie at a stretch, but on getting to the Needles Mail Stables I was so hot and tired that I went in and asked permission to have a rest. The man in charge, a bright blue-eyed, intelligent, manly looking German willingly granted this.

On getting into conversation with him, he told me that the shooting there was the best in South Australia and asked me to stop and have some sport on the morrow. I jumped at the offer and then jumped on a horse and rode into McCallum's to buy 4 lbs. No.2. shot. He has a wife and little boy. I had a fair shakedown and we arranged to get up at 4.15 next day.

Monday morning then saw us up just about daybreak. We had a single-barrelled muzzleloader each. It proved to be a pretty cool day. A walk of a mile brought us to the Coorong. We walked quietly along with a sand ridge between us and the sea till we saw, in a channel between the beach and an island an immense number of teal swimming about and feeding. Jack said "Bother it, they're all too far out"; but I noticed a flock of twenty or thirty quite close to the bank. Just opposite there the sand ridge got almost flush with the plain, but on it were two small stunted bushes. We crawled carefully along and got safely up to these bushes and one lay down behind each. In whispers we agreed that I was to fire at them first and Jack was to take them as they rose. I look up; they are still feeding quietly, though a fairly long way off. I let drive into the bunch and then wait to hear another shot; but his gun was only half cocked. The teal were up in a perfect cloud, leaving two on the water, one wounded, the other dead. My companion follows the former and captures it on the island. We now wade across to this island, go round it and take up our station on a ledge of rocks running out in the direction of another pretty island half a mile distant. Dummies are placed at intervals across to this island to drive the wild fowl towards where we are placed. Just as we get there an immense flock - some thousands there must have been - of snipe (cobblers) fly past and I knock over three. A great many more flocks pass, but I only succeed in shooting one more and my companion gets one. They were a tall white bird with long red beak and long pink legs.

    The waterfowl further up the Coorong, in the shallow water, were a sight to see: teal in countless myriads, mountain ducks in small flocks every here and there - swans - and great bands of pelicans and droves of cobblers. We now left the rocks and went back to the mainland. We gradually edged down the sea and several times stalked numbers of cobblers feeding and running about in the shallow water, but failed to get a shot. At the end of a sort of little headland were four teal. I got to within thirty yards of them by keeping behind an old dyke; I fired and - they all four flew off.

    We went for breakfast into a Mailman's, whose wife is the blacks' food dispenser. After it, as Jack had to go home, I went on on my own account. Out of three cobblers I knocked over one and then waded right across to the Snake Island, mentioned as the island towards which the ledge of rocks ran. I turned to the right and walked all round the island without seeing anything till I came to the southern portion of it. I did some arduous stalking and bagged three more cobblers. If I'd had a breachloader I could have hit several more.

For dinner I ate those two beautiful stump teal and immediately afterwards went off to the ledge of rocks before spoken of. Here we sat all the afternoon, half in the water and half out, and the teal flew over us in perfect swarms. Jack knocks over one first and then got another and then two more. All this time I had been banging away, but though I could see that all I tried at were very severely hit, none would drop. At length, by a magnificent shot, out of two that flew over, one ten feet in front of the other, I felled one (the last though I must confess I aimed at his mate). I then got my eye in and brought down, out of a large flock, a teal certainly not more than five yards from the lucky intended one. After numbers of unsuccessful shots I get disgusted and swap guns with my mate. I ram down two charges of powder and a double dose of shot. An unusually large mob fly past. I shut my eyes and let drive. Though the gun kicks I have the satisfaction of seeing two drop, one of them winged. My companion seems astounded. "However did you do that" he said, "Oh, I just waited till I got two in a line and then bagged both. It's an easy enough thing to do when you know how", said I, drawing myself up in the pride of conscious superiority. He gets another and then we make home. A crack sportsman could have bagged forty or fifty.

Tuesday was a fine day for travelling nice and cloudy. I got away by ten. Dense mallee scrub is on both sides of the road for some miles. You lose sight of the Coorong on leaving the Needles -- if indeed you could see it from the Needles. The road is the best road for a pedestrian that I have seen on my trip. A beautiful pipeclay. The country gets more open as you get along, uninteresting forest taking the place of the rich coloured mallee. A little way from Meningie you get a fine view. The Lake Albert stretching away out of sight to the front of you and the road runs right through the township parallel to the straight side of the lake.

A walk of six and a half miles to an arm of the sea... saw house to right; had tea, bed and breakfast for three shillings .... day hot .... five miles through forest, two miles across flat, came to house, dinner. Fearfully weary walk. Left W. Bay, through forest, round lake ..

10th February.

The township (Meningie) consisting of a few scattered houses on both sides of the mainroad, lies at your feet. The water of Lake Albert tasted delicious after the hard water I had been drinking for the last three weeks. I sat down on the end of the jetty where the steamer from Milano lands her passengers, and had some lunch. For six miles after leaving Meningie my course was due north beside Lake Albert, over perfectly flat country. Four blacks I met, three men and a woman, the former in front, the woman a black-bearded thin-legged hag, carrying an immense quantity of blankets, rugs etc. At the Willtowa swamp, which I crossed by a made piece of road, I saw another almost incredible mass of wild fowl. The water was just black with teal from within thirty yards of the road to as far as the eye could reach. I saw also an immense number of native companions. I followed the telegraph line for two miles further through marshy country covered with stunted bushes, and then I saw the house I was bound for half a mile off the track to the right. It was an accommodation house kept by a Mr. Telland, and I did fare sumptuously, bullock's liver and mashed potatoes for tea, with delicious bread and butter, and only charged one shilling.

11th February.

Fearfully hot; washed some socks in the morning, so couldn't get away till 10 a.m. For the first five miles, my walk was through the bush still in a northerly direction to cut off a triangular piece of land which separates Lakes Albert and Alexandrina. I was on high ground when I first saw the water, but then the road rapidly got lower, and for two miles till I got to a farm house I was walking over undulating grassy plains. It was a dreary tramp, the thirteen miles into Wellington, firstly through marshy tracts, then over grassy flats, then by a heavy sandy road, then round the lake, through the township, and by a made road across the swamp to the punt. The charge for being ferried across was one penny. The Wellington Hotel is an instance of a house built on the sand, in fact it is half buried by that material. The Murray, I was told, is one hundred yards wide at its mouth.

12th February.

Wellington is sixty five miles from Adelaide, and I hope to do the distance in either two or three days. As there is constant mail communication between the two places, there is of course a metal road. Ten miles wretchedly uninteresting travelling over flats and by the northern extremity of Lake Alexandrina brought me to a public-house at Mulgondawa, kept by a Dame - Darnke by name. Ten miles further on I passed through Langhorne's Bridge township, and remember being struck with a shop kept by Berry & Smith, and after another ten miles, a great part of which was walked in the dark, I got into Strathalbyn at 10 p.m., and made for the Victoria Hotel, kept by a widow. She was in a great state of anxiety about a little girl who had gone astray, yet managed to give me a good tea.

13th February.

The church bells were rung last night, and every male person in Strathalbyn turned out to look for the child. They thoroughly searched the Angas river, on which the town is situated, groped into every corner and looked into every well in the place. About 9 o' clock this morning a horseman came in with the news that the child had turned up safe at Port Victor. It had been playing about, and had fallen to sleep in a van, was unnoticed by the driver, and hence the catastrophe. Strathalbyn is a very picturesque town, with handsome churches and hotel. The newspaper is the *Southern Argus*, and there is a population of about one thousand five hundred. I had a glorious walk, though the sun was very powerful, through country beautifully timbered on both sides of the road.

Macclesfield is delightfully situated, eight miles from Strathalbyn. Six miles further on is Echunga, celebrated for the gold mines in the vicinity, also in a glorious position. I had my dinner at the Hagem Arms. I could only get eight miles nearer Adelaide, I was so tired; so I stopped at the Aldgate Pump, where Mr. Myers has an excellent hotel. He had some discriminative power, and treated me like a gentleman, though I was but a tramp.

14th February: Saturday.

Today I completed my walk, wished to get into Adelaide by 12 o'clock, so left at 8 a.m. Being in good condition I frequently ran. The scenery is, of course, too well known for me to spoil by attempting to describe it. I was in ecstasies all the way. In fact, from Strathalbyn the walk has been almost equal to the sublime scenery in the Cape Otway forest. I got some lime juice at the celebrated *Eagle on the Hill*, and arrived in Adelaide at the Post Office at three minutes before twelve. My whole walk has been six hundred and fifty-two miles, or the way I went seven hundred and fifty-two. I loafed about the town for an hour or two, and in the afternoon went down the oval to see Jarvis play. As I seated myself in the grand stand a general titter passed through the crowd, and everybody tried to be funny at my expense, just because I had on a flannel cricketing shirt, perhaps a little dirty, old serge breeches, a green cap, leggings, old boots and a knapsack. One pertinacious old fool was very inquisitive, and would have it that I had been down two years before with sheep, and that he had seen me. I have now finished both my walk and my diary, so I will shut up.

Affie Jarvis, South Australian wicket-keeper, toured with the Australians, 1880.

The Traveller: Across The Australian Continent On Foot

It had long been a wish of mine to cross Australia. Lying in Port Mackay with two crippled knees, I first resolved to do the journey on foot. When I heard on all sides of the long stages between stations and the impossibility of travelling without at least two horses, I decided to go alone, and when everyone croaked to me that the blacks would kill me, if the floods did not drown me, I swore I would go unarmed.

Fever I had to fear as well as the blacks; quinine would be required to combat the former; a telescope might forewarn me of the latter. My telescope was stolen from me in Cooktown; my quinine, by accident, was thrown away at Thursday Island. Of all things none was more likely to be useful than a compass, yet mine was utterly destroyed in New Guinea. What could I argue from these things, but that fever would pass me unharming, blacks would never endanger my life, nor would I ever be in a situation from which there was no escape but by the use of the compass.

At Normanton, when I gave out my intention of strolling to Melbourne, people professed to think me mad. The rainy season was impending, and many signs, especially the comet [i.e. the Great Comet of 1882], pointed to its being earlier than usual. "How reckless," said one; "so insane," put in another; "it's suicide," added a third. The elderly landlady of the hotel grew eloquent as to the dangers which awaited me. She was no cur [cowardly person] she assured me, but she wouldn't be game to tackle such a walk.

Fearing an attack of nervousness I hurried out of Normanton to a hotel 15 miles on the road to Cloncurry. Five teams were camped here. It rained with unpromising severity the latter part of two days, and as the next house was 75 miles away I had just to wait patiently.

On Friday evening the 22nd December, the sky was clear for the first time, and starting at once I was 30 miles on my way before it came on to rain again. The teams hesitated, and have been there ever since I fancy. This long stage is much dreaded by the carriers. It lies through country lightly timbered with the gutta-percha tree [a genus of tropical trees native to northern Australia], the stunted bastard box, and the coolibah, a district said to swarm with blacks, and annually subject to inundation.

When I was half-way through there came on a violent tempest of wind and rain. The track became a bog and the knapsack got so sodden with water that I groaned under its weight. It was not safe to rest. The accounts I had heard of the track when flooded made me tremble to sit down, so I wearily struggled on through water and mud up to my knees, forgetting the dangers of this dismal, gloomy country in the fatigue of walking. Suddenly the wind died away, the sun shone out through the clouds, the rain stopped, and in little while I came to where no rain had fallen at all. It had been merely a local storm.

The following morning I came to two huts and a stockyard, the cattle station of Veno Park. Two stages of 25 miles each through country where monotonous flatness is occasionally relieved by richly wooded sandhills, bring you the first to a cattle station, the second to a public-house. Spear Creek which has been on your left hand, is now lost sight of. The Sanby is crossed, and you are on that immense plain which stretches to the Flinders River.

Between the Cockatoo waterhole, 3 miles beyond the Sanby, and a low hill called Fort Brown, within 3 miles of the Flinders there is a dead waterless flat, almost bare of trees, which is buried some feet under water during the rainy season. Carriers tell me 30 feet, and I can well believe it, for the high gums on the banks of the Flinders River have drift timber in their very topmost branches.

I had a mate when crossing this plain, an old man who sought my company out of nervousness. He was mounted on a poor wretched moke which had a fistula between its shoulders that was sickening to look at. Yet he was very proud of his horse and was quite disgusted the only bid he could get for horse, saddle and bridle when he put him up for sale, was 10s. Locomotion was so painful to the horse that hobbles would have been superfluous. His only fault in the eye of his owner was that he was not a mare.

When buying flour for my mate and myself I asked him how much should we require; 6 lb, he replied. "Surely," said I , "6 lb of flour will not be enough for you and me for three days" - we were 31 miles from the next house – but he begged of me to trust him for that. Borrowing the loan of the kitchen he baked a damper of the weight and hardness of a stone. We had no knife strong enough to cut it.

I constantly passed teams now till I got into Cloncurry. Water and grass were abundant and with the £30 a ton for the 250 miles from the Norman River to Cloncurry they had made satisfactory profits. I went some miles off the road to see the first sheep station. The Guy country seems ill adapted for the sheep, though horses and cattle thrive wonderfully, but here, over 200 miles from the coast, the sheep does splendidly on the open downs with Gidya ridges, which stretch away to the N.W. of Cloncurry.

Between the Norman River and Cloncurry I saw neither kangaroos, emus nor wild dogs, though the latter abound. There were native turkeys in scores, and every pool of water swarmed with wild fowl. Kites were more plentiful than crows, and you never stopped for a meal but the trees near became grey with kites waiting for you to leave that they might swoop down upon the scraps.

The wretched blacks are shot without mercy. One night I was at a station, whose owner is said to have shot more blacks than any two men in Queensland, when the mailman came in and reported that he had seen a black prowling about the stockyard. Loading his rifle Mr. -- at once sallied out after him, but came back in an hour quite disappointed that, though he could pick up the tracks by the stockyard, it was too dark to follow them. Alligators are said to swarm in Spear Creek, as the Norman River is called above Normanton; I hesitate to give dimensions of the largest that has been seen.

Cloncurry is situated in a slightly elevated upland, in the centre of a pan-shaped depression, surrounded by a rim of low hills. The adjacent country is very rich in minerals. Payable gold has been got here for many years. Bismuth, antimony and manganese are found. There is a hill of iron, and a supposed large deposit of coal; but copper is the most abundant of its minerals. There is a mine of nearly virgin copper, so pure indeed as to be at present, owing to the abundance of firewood, unworkable. This mine lately changed hands for £26,000, so there seems good reason for believing that the copper has a real existence.

From Cloncurry my route lay to Winton. A publican in town kindly drew me a diagram by which I was to find my way to a hut on the McKinlay River, 10½ miles distant. That map I keep as a curiosity. A distance of 9 miles was made to appear twice as long as one of 22 miles, a trifling inaccuracy which caused me unnecessary anxiety and torture. The first night I could not sleep from fear that I had taken a wrong turning. In the morning I started to go 35 miles without knowing whether there was water on the track, or even water where I was making to. My water-bag holds two quarts and a half, but the day was so hot – the thermometer registered 130 degree in the shade of the hut I refer to – that by midday, although I had hardly wet my mouth, the water was all evaporated.

Still I kept moving, but at half-past four I felt knocked up. It came upon me most suddenly. Without any warning I was seized by an irresistible desire to throw off all my clothes. I had no wish in the world but to lie down. I camped under a tree. The anxiety of mind, for it was but a chance if water was within 13 miles of me, added to my thirst, and I suffered torments. All through the night I lay naked on my back, my tongue contracted to a point, my body hot and feverish, my brain reeling.

Just as day dawned I staggered to my feet, but which way was I to turn, to the right or the left? In a brief intermission of my confusion I recollected that I had turned off to the tree to the right; but during the night I had got my head where my feet should have been, and I actually tried to pick up the track by walking away from it. But Providence watched over me, and set me on my way. I was so dazed that the track became more blurred and indistinct every minute.

A wide plain now stretched before me, and a belt of timber at its further end gave me hope. I reached the creek and threw down my knapsack, and followed up and down the sandy bed for a weary distance, but it was as dry as the Sahara. On again, and another plain, with another belt of timber was to cheer or disappoint me. The creek was drier looking and sandier than the first one.

I was throwing myself down in despair, when my eyes lit on a beautiful pool of water under the shade of a weeping ti-tree. The reaction quite unnerved me. I rested and drank all day. The mailman came up in the evening and gave me information about the country ahead. The contrast struck me forcibly. There were richly grassed instead of arid plains; creeks no longer dry and sandy, but sparling with water, and plantations of timber, healthy and vigorous, not a parched and stunted forest. The twin parallel channels of the William River meander through a country as beautiful as an English park. Then a vast plain extends to the horizon, where dancing grotesquely in the sun, is the timber marking the course of the Fullarton River.

Two days walk from here is the McKinlay River, which drains an immense area of rolling downs. I was tracing up this river, cutting from one point of timber to another, and wondering whether the hut was above or below me, when I saw a man on horseback driving cattle. I drew nearer and nearer to him, and long before I could see his face, I recognised the wild war song which had so often inspirited me in my voyage to the islands. This was a young Kanaka, a kindly nice lad, from Metaiva, beguiled from his home – one of the most beautiful islands of Polynesia – to tend cattle, to do fencing, to mix with gins, amid all the sultry dreariness and cheerlessness of the most utterly wretched district of the Never-Never.

The manager of this cattle station was in Cloncurry, and the South Sea Islander was in sole charge. I was taken very unwell when with him, and for three days the Kanaka showed me the greatest kindness and attention. Leaving now the McKinlay River and steering diagonally over to its first sandy billabong, I traced it up till I came to an out station. In this stage of 30 miles I was two days without eating anything, during which I suffered much from thirst.

The next stage was 25 miles over the ranges in which the Diamantina takes its source. The heat was something fearful, there was an entire absence of animal life, a faintly marked track which turned and twisted to every point of the compass and continually ran out, and no water, though billabongs and sandy creeks were crossed by the hundred. The only excitement that sustained me in my weakness was the fear of blacks – the wild Kalkadoons who are so greatly feared in the hills.

At the head-waters of the Diamantina, a sheep station was being formed where the countless billabongs resolve themselves into one of the finest rivers in Australia, a river which shall perpetuate the name of Lady Bowen. The Diamantina from its source trends away to the north-east, and then bends round in the shape of a shepherd's crook. I was on it for 113 miles, having it for 56 miles on my left, then crossing it at Dagworth station, and having it on my right for 57 miles, till its junction with the Western at Elderslie, one of Sir Samuel Wilson's properties. Both here and at Dagworth there was immense activity. Two or three years hence they intend having 30,000 sheep at Elderslie and a proportionate number on Dagworth.

Fencing, tank sinking and building were proceeding with marvellous activity; wages are very high; any unskilled man can earn 30s. or 35s. a week; he will be well fed, as a vegetable garden is now an essential part of a large Queensland station. I was out of the country where men are content to exist on salt beef and damper. The money spent by the squatters hereabouts chiefly finds it way into the public-houses of Winton, a rising township on the Pelican Waterholes, near the Western River, placed on a high flat, with not a tree near it.

The Kalkadoon tribe, who were massacred in 1884.

The telegraph line is being extended from here to Cloncurry. Vinden station, another magnificent sheep run, is 15 miles out of Winton. Fifty miles further is Evershan station. Then there is a break in the open downs, and you pass through a lot of Gidya scrub [scrubby acacia or wattle], country through Maneroo station to the Thompson River – at this early stage, a trickle of peculiar white water which I stepped across.

The day after crossing the Thompson I was overtaken by an old gentleman on horseback whose companionship I found so agreeable that we travelled on together for 75 miles. He was a toothless darkie, a native of the Gold Coast of Africa, a cook by profession, and one of the kindest, most considerate men it has been my lot to meet with. He would ride on ahead and open the gates that I might not break my stride. He would stint himself of water if the day were hot that I might have the more. And this how we fell out. We had to go one day 25 miles carrying water. Though parched with thirst he would not take his share. Not to be outdone I also refused any water, and being annoyed I vowed that we must part. I am glad of an opportunity to record my sense of this darkie's kindness. John Smith was his name, and he was the first black man ever seen in Iceland, having been there when a boy on board a Dutch man-of-war which was taking Prince Henry of the Netherlands round the world.

The Thompson River we left some distance on our right, two stations being situated on creeks running into it. On the Bimerah Creek is Bimerah station, which, like all Fairbairn's stations, is being rapidly improved on a princely scale. Twelve miles further there was a sudden change. The water in the Emu Creek was stinking; the fish were rotting in the mud, and the crows were in hundreds. Up to this creek, grass had been in abundance. Not till I was overtaken by rain, 250 miles further on, did I again come to any.

Now I had to pass through the downs and Gidya scrub, which had been the characteristics of the country for the last 600 miles, till in three days I walked into the township of Jundah. There is a store here, a saddler and public-house, and there will be other houses shortly. I will chiefly remember it, because of the splendid dam of water in the Thomson and because of the interesting fact that every man in the township was more or less drunk. All were lost in drunken amazement at my prodigious walk.

I was now an experienced swagman. My swag was carried New Zealand, or knapsack fashion. The tucker, spare shoes, socks and shirts, some reading matter and a hammock, the matches, baking powder and canvas basil were rolled up in a single blanket, and the whole then enveloped in a strip of oilcloth and borne on my back, being kept by straps passing over the shoulders. In this way only could I secure the untrammelled use of my arms.

The swag was seldom less than 20lb; above this its weight varied according to the distance I had to carry tucker. I seldom travelled at night; the heat of the day never troubled me. Indeed it is my favourite boast that I have yet to see the day that is too hot for me. My own dress was cabbage-tree hat, flannel shirt, and tweed trousers, afterwards replaced by moleskins, and a knife belt and sheaf. Boots I wore two sizes too large, and as I always cut the stiffening out of the back before using them, I escaped that soreness of heel which has troubled me on my former walks.

Upon arriving at a station I went straight to the store, bought what rations I required, and camped by the most convenient water. The greatest hospitality was always shown to me at stations where I was known, but I made it a rule to be independent of all help as possible. When I had decided to camp I spread the oil-cloth, and having lit a fire, put on my salt beef to boil in the billy. By the time it was done and the quart of tea made, I had a Johnny cake or flatjack ready for cooking on the raked out coals. The former differ only in the size and are distinct from a damper in that they are cooked on the hot embers, whereas a damper is baked in the hot ashes with the hot embers outside. No wood that I have seen can equal the Gidya for giving the very ash and ember most valuable to us. A johnny cake made with baking powder is a most delicious scone – the very best baking powder is Eno's fruit salt.

Of course I did not restrict myself to these two articles of diet. I would vary them with apples and rice, sage or arrowroot, and occasionally with beef tea and potatoes. Preserved potatoes, when prepared in the water in which you have boiled your meat, are most delicious. Soda is an excellent baking powder; the johnny cake becomes a beautiful yellow, so that you can imagine you are eating bread made with milk, butter and eggs. At the stores – every station has its store – flour was 9d. to 1s. per pound, rice 1s., apples and potatoes 1s. 6d., and meat, though most of the stations do not charge for it, was 3d. to 6d. a pound for salt beef.

But to return. No one in Jundah could give me any lucid information where water might be in the next 65 miles. It is the uncertainty which predisposes to the fever of the palate. With the river in sight on my left, and never more than 5 or 6 miles from me, I knew that I could always get water by turning off to it. This, then, was well enough. But the least intoxicated man in Jundah was most positive that there was one stage absolutely without water for 18 miles. He had offered to fight anyone who contradicted him, yet his statement passed unchallenged. I therefore inferred he was speaking the truth. If, then, I had been thirsty, had turned off 5 miles to water and found none this 18 miles, it would have gone hard with me.

The Longreach mail arrives at Jundah Post Office.

As it happened, my anxiety was uncalled for. At several places in the 65 miles, cattle tracks crossed the path, and by following them I was always brought to water, but so stale and filthy that it gave me severe gripping pains in the stomach which interfered much with my walking. For a greater part of this distance my way lay through a corner of a vast cattle run owned by two men, and in extent larger than Yorkshire and Durham.

On the 15th of February I came to the most interesting river in Australia. Fifteen miles above this, the Thompson had joined the Barcoo. Wading waist deep through the combined stream, I paused half way to admire the glorious reaches of the river opened up above and below me, and the high banks crowned with magnificent timber. Every description of wild fowl floated idly on the unruffled surface of the current, and it was idleness which reigned supreme over the encampment of blacks in the timber on the opposite bank.

I was so delighted with seeing Cooper's Creek at last that, despite an empty tucker bag, I must need camp for the night on its margin. Seven miles from the crossing I reached a cattle station, and 28 miles further another. The sky now became overcast, the sun was rarely visible, and everything foreboded rain. I rested a day or two and went on. A slight drizzle fell persistently. Not heavy enough to keep me awake, it made all my things sodden. There was no sun to dry them, nor had I sufficient patience to steam them before a fire.

Once I lost my box of matches, and calling at a house to replenish them, was given as a favour 19 lucifers. These had to last me two days sleeping out in the meantime. I cannot imagine any severer trial for one's nerves than when hungry, with no food cooked, nor any house within a day's walk, to have to light a fire in wind or rain with your last match.

On the 23rd of February the Thargomindah and Windorah mailman served me a dirty trick. While I was camped for lunch he and another man came up to me, both well mounted, and driving pack horses. It was a hot, sultry, thirsty day, and I had a larger stock of water than usual, having filled my two quart billy as well as my water bag. These men asked me for a drink, and, before I could stop them, they had emptied my billy of all but a cupful, though they were within 2 miles of water on horseback, while I was over 28 from it on foot. I made it a rule of my walk never to ask or accept a drink from any traveller, whether on foot or horseback. It gave me satisfaction to be independent even in this.

The same evening of my meeting with the mailman, a foot traveller overtook me and we camped together. We made an excellent breakwind, lit a roaring fire, for we were once more in Gidya country with abundance of firewood, and calmly settled ourselves for the night. But we were not long asleep before the slight drizzle which had forewarned us was succeeded by a heavy pelting rain that knew no ceasing. One could hardly believe the effect of that rain. In the morning our camp was on the only dry ground within sight. For 15 miles we did not see land. The track was a clearly defined channel between bushes. The creeks were running into a very strong current, and we were so often in water up to our armpits that I travelled with nothing but my shirt.

We reached shelter, there to be detained for three days. It rained for seventy-six hours at one stretch. In five days, nine inches and thirty points fell. Dams were burst everywhere. The whole country into Thargomindah was become a vast series of swamps and flooded creeks. Buckling to it, every danger vanished at my approach. Wading through swamps and swimming creeks with long distances to carry food, I yet experienced no fatigue; the dash of excitement kept it away. Where the swamp extended for miles it was but natural that in threading my way among the trees, with no guide but the sun, and water often to my breast, I should wander from the track, but a wide cast on the dry ground would as surely discover it to me.

When the water was in motion, centipedes in hundreds and an occasional snake constantly floated across the path in unpleasant proximity. The snakes I saw in my walk were more varied than numerous. On the red Mulga ridges I killed several Mulga snakes – a finely marked brown snake nearly 6 feet in length. When I was at the head waters of the Diamantina, a black passed me, trailing after him a snake 9 feet 6 inches long, and as thick as a cable. It is a kind of rock python, which often attains a length of 12 or 15 feet. The black would have me to believe that it was not deadly.

It is a man's duty to kill every snake he can. I have killed the brown snake, the tiger snake, the poor harmless carpet snake, and a black snake with a blue belly. There were many I had no means of identifying, not the least interesting being an active little fellow, which was disturbed by my coming, and commenced to wriggle about in a most fantastic way. Just as I turned away for a stick it made one spring off the track and vanished down a hold not large enough to introduce your two smallest fingers. Many anecdotes of snakes were told me. People so unkindly take advantage of one's credulous inexperience.

The Bulloo I crossed in a boat; a deep wade then put me on the track to Hungerford. At Thargomindah I had laid in such a large supply of flour and beef that for 75 miles I was absolutely independent of everyone. Timber and water were abundant. By this time I had trained myself to do with very little water. I could walk 25 miles without wetting my lips. The Corellas flock to water at sundown, the thirsty traveller need but be guided by them, and he will infallibly be brought to water. The Paroo was greatly swollen. I had been told to be careful, as the bed of the river is thickly timbered with the Yapunyah.

The stream was not less than half a mile wide, and you cannot see the opposite bank till quite close to it. But caution was unnecessary. I walked slap in, and crossed without difficulty. Hungerford is across the river. The boundary between New South Wales and Queensland passes through the centre of town. The hotel is

The Cobb & Co mail crossing the Paroo River in flood.

in Queensland, where the licence is less; the store is in New South Wales, where there is free trade. I had done with Queensland. Drinks were now 6d., and mutton was to take the place of beef.

In crossing the Paroo, 20 miles below Hungerford, I waded in a careless way into a stream, with my heavy swag on my back. Gradually it got deeper; it came over my waist; it reached my breast, my chin then was in the water; the next moment I went out of my depth altogether. The current in among the lignum bushes was very strong, and being impeded with my swag and boots I was a long time floundering about before I could get into my depth. The experience was of use to me. I stripped and found a passage among the trees; then, returning for my things, I swam over with them in comfort.

Not till I was 100 miles below Hungerford did I overtake the flood waters of the Paroo and wade through the last of the swamps. There were public houses now every 10 or 20 miles into Wilcannia. Away out in that wretched country of clay pans and sand ridges, with its uninteresting scrub, its vast flats of saltbush and occasional stretches of barren hills, I suddenly came on a beautiful lake which wandered away to the east till its outer margin was hidden.

For a little while I felt enthusiastic about the country I was in, but having to toil for some hours through heavy sand my misplaced enthusiasm was turned to ridicule. The scene constantly opening before me seemed the very incarnation of dreary desolation. These days were very lonely. Weak and fagged, and badly in need of a spell, I could not rest till I was in Wilcannia. I got in an hour after the telegraph had closed on Easter Monday; it was Wednesday before I had the means of buying any food.

With no money in my pocket, and camped on the flat below the hospital, where those vagrants who have knocked down their cheques in the hells of this town rest till recuperated enough to start away with their swag, my experience of Wilcannia was not a cheerful one. Another young fellow was in a similar predicament to myself, but he knew a Chinese cook at one of the hotels, and twice sponged a supper. On the second evening another of us camped there, was put in the lockup and got a fortnight. Another had been living on this flat for months; no one knew how he lived; he hadn't a sixpence.

On the Wednesday I got money and gave a farewell *al fresco* feed to all the tramps and vagabonds, after which I left on the 70 mile track. At the end of the 70 miles is Mount Manaro station, situated in the hollow of the enclosing hills. The way lies through vast clay flats of saltbush and mallee, interspersed with edges of mulga, boree, leopard woods and sandal wood. The walking is heavy, and there is one stage of 23 miles without water. Above Ivanhoe the country is comparatively picturesque. Immediately after leaving it I got into the endless saltbush plains, the few clumps of box and pine on which can be seen such an incredible distance. The large box which gives its name to the One Tree Plain can be seen 20 miles off. There are public-houses every 10 or 12 miles. The landlady of one of them poses in Melbourne society as a squatter's wife. Up here she is known as the scrub turkey.

I travelled now very rapidly. From Hay I passed through Deniliquin, Echuca, Rochester, Elmore, Heathcote and Kilmore, reaching Melbourne on the 21st of April. While in my own colony it was a perfect picnic. Instead of immense tracts of country owned by one man, and given up to sheep, there were a succession of beautiful little farms, each with its haystack, its neat little cottage, its substantial fence, and its scene of vigorous activity. Ploughing was in full swing, clearing and grubbing.

The beautiful hilly country, seemingly so fertile, and supporting so excellent a class of people, pleased me beyond measure. Certainly, I thought, my colony may be the smallest, but it is the healthiest and most beautiful of them all.

This fact I have left to the last. I came 1700 miles through the interior of Australia without seeing a kangaroo. My only objection to writing this account of my walk was a natural one. If it had never been written many people might think that I had done something wonderful. They will read this and and see that any one who cared to take the trouble and give up four months of his time could have done the walk more quickly than I did, more easily, and with less discomfort to himself.

One Tree Plain Hotel.

www.ingramcontent.com/pod-product-compliance
Lightning Source LLC
Chambersburg PA
CBHW050820090426
42737CB00021B/3454